The Mental Game

*For our families, especially Ute and Agi*

Daniel Memmert • Stefan Leiner

# THE MENTAL
# GAME

## Cognitive Training, Creativity, and Game Intelligence in Tennis

MEYER & MEYER SPORT

British Library of Cataloguing in Publication Data
A catalogue record for this book is available from the British Library

Original title: *Tennisspiele werden im Kopf entschieden*, © 2020 by Meyer & Meyer Verlag, Aachen, Germany

**The Mental Game**
Maidenhead: Meyer & Meyer Sport (UK) Ltd., 2023
ISBN: 978-1-78255-258-1

© 2023 by Meyer & Meyer Sport (UK) Ltd.
Aachen, Auckland, Beirut, Cairo, Cape Town, Dubai, Hägendorf, Hong Kong, Indianapolis, Maidenhead, Manila, New Delhi, Singapore, Sydney, Tehran, Vienna
 Member of the World Sports Publishers' Association (WSPA), www.w-s-p-a.org

Printed by Print Consult GmbH, Munich, Germany
Printed in Slovakia.

ISBN: 978-1-78255-258-1
Email: info@m-m-sports.com
www.thesportspublisher.com

# CONTENTS

# FOREWORD

## FROM A TRAINER'S POINT OF VIEW

*"There is no replacement for practice and a good teacher."*

*–Richard Strozzi-Heckler*

*"Practise is the thing we do to be faithful, not successful."*

*–Jeff Salzman, Daily Evolver podcast*

Success is what we all strive for. Whether we are working with children and young people, whether we are involved in popular sports, whether we train professional athletes, or whether we are athletes ourselves, the thing that unites us is the intention to succeed.

I've been closely involved with professional tennis for 30 years, playing on the tour in the 1990s and having a few matches against the big names of that time. I also played in the national tennis league for a good 10 years. When my motivation and inspiration waned and I developed other interests, I changed sides and worked as a trainer and coach from then on. Among other things, I was the national coach and team manager of the German Davis Cup team.

My heart was attached to international professional tennis from the very beginning. And so, I have now been working in this field for 20 years. I train professionals, traveling with them from tournament to tournament around the world. I have also advised and coached people in the middle third of their lives, who are professionally active in performance contexts, on health-related topics for a good 10 years.

In the last 20 years on tour, I have been at about 90% of all Grand Slam tournaments. I have been able to observe many tennis legends up close as a coach, often as a neutral observer in the stands and sometimes as the coach of an athlete who was competing against one of the greats. All of this has contributed to a wealth of experience that has developed in me over the last 30 years in elite tennis.

A lot has changed! One major difference between my time as a professional in the 1990s and today is the specialization and professionalization of the training process. There is much more detail and precision. The differences between the best in the world are minimal, which a look at the statistical evaluations always proves.

Science has been taken more seriously and consulted more often in three essential areas: technical/tactical, athletic, and mental. New ways and more effective methods are continually sought. While in the 1990s there was usually one coach for everything, today it is necessary and natural to work with a team. Physiotherapists and athletic coaches are essential companions to the professionals and provide feedback for the coaches. External IT providers now produce technical and tactics analyses and make coaching work much more accessible.

In the mental/psychological field, cooperation with sports psychologists and performance coaches has long been socially acceptable, with the pointed comment that the coaches themselves are not yet so comfortable with making use of these opportunities to reflect on their actions.

To increase the probability of succeeding—and there is nothing we can do other than try to influence probabilities—it is important to keep turning to sports science. And it is precisely the mental, cognitive area—which is constantly pointed to by so many coaches and athletes as a crucial success factor in top-level sport—that needs our increased attention.

- What are the findings in cognitive science?

- What do the studies say? What don't they say?

- Do they support the intuitive and often not rationally explainable trainer action?

- Is there anything new and valuable here for sports?

- Does it remain a difficult-to-understand theory or is it possible and realistic to implement in daily coaching work?

This is exactly where this excellent, in-depth book by Daniel Memmert and Stefan Leiner steps in.

But before I turn to the substantive part of the book, I would like to make some personal comments and put the concept of success into a larger context.

In the beginning, I said that we are all united by the pursuit of success. Seen in this light, that is the lowest common denominator. However, if we think about how we define success for ourselves and what meaning it has for us, we will sometimes differ significantly in these descriptions.

Our definition of success depends on many factors: our view of the world; what being human means to us; what is fundamentally important to us; where our aspirations take us; what values guide us; how we can distance ourselves from ourselves and turn to our counterpart, whether individual athlete or team; whether we have the good of the whole in mind. Our responses to these ideas will lead to different definitions of success in sport. First, the simple step of differentiating perspectives can be helpful and useful here.

*I, we, it.* These are basic perspectives we can take toward any event or aspect of reality. We find these pronouns in all major languages. They mark the perspective from which perception is formulated. The more consciously I can adopt them, the more differentiated my perception will become and the more information can be gathered to solve questions concerning the training and tournament process.

In our time, we still tend quite strongly towards a benefit-oriented, materialistic, external world view. While this is often helpful, it remains only a partial truth. Every trainer can easily understand this scenario: You have planned a training session systematically, according to scientific knowledge. And then you meet with the athlete and you sense that something is not right. There is something in the air, an atmosphere that, if we are sensitive to it, demands something different from us. If I only have my expert knowledge at my disposal on these days, I won't get very far.

Being able to take the "I" perspective means being able to switch from external perception to my inner space, my inner experience: Anger about the training session planned in vain might become palpable. A resistance to hearing the athlete's old stories again, an unwillingness to react flexibly to them. Many buttons could be pushed in me and lead to inappropriate reactions. Developing self-awareness for this and having rituals and routines available to bring me into a present, centered, calm state are qualities that the "me" perspective would be about. This cultivation of presence as a coach is inextricably linked to my effectiveness.

And very basic questions also have their place here:

- What sustains and nourishes stress, failure?

- How do I manage stress and recovery?

- Where are the moments of exuberance, joy, and serenity in my life?

- Where do I need development?

- Where are my blind spots?

- Am I aware of my life principles and virtues?

- What are the deep-seated premises that underlie my decisions?

In the "we" perspective, it's less about my inner experience and more about turning toward my counterpart and creating empathy and goodwill towards the athletes. Empathy for what the situation needs answers to the following questions:

- Clarity of address?

- Can I take myself back and listen empathetically?

- Can I allow conflicts, which are necessary for development?

- Can I deal with them constructively and benevolently?

- Do I communicate clearly what I demand as a trainer and where my limits are?

- What are no-gos in a collaboration?

- Can I distinguish between my interpretations and projections in my perception of the other?

- Can I inspire and convey hope and confidence to the athlete? In the sense that it will be a difficult road, but we'll get there!

- Do we create an atmosphere in which we would like to have trained?

- Would we commit ourselves as coaches?

The "it" perspective is that this is the field of (sports) science, technical literature, externally oriented, measurable facts, intelligent match analyses that explain through differ-entiated statistics why someone won a tennis match and what can be derived from this for the training process.

The qualities of "me" and "we" are crucial success factors, and we should definitely develop these as trainers. These are skills that I consider to be equally important in us trainers, compared to externally oriented expertise. Well-trained in these skills, I will be able to use my trainer know-how much more effectively. Ultimately, it should be clear that change can only be achieved through certain states of consciousness. To be able to create these in me and to promote them in others is very helpful in trainer work. In the training of coaches, at least in tennis, much more emphasis could be placed on this.

For me, the ability to be able to take these different perspectives in a situationally appropriate way, to practice and play with them, is part of the basic equipment of every coach. If we want to work successfully, we need to be deeply anchored in our intentions and visions, we need sustainable routines for our own resilience and the ability to inspire others, and we should act out of a deep goodwill towards our athletes. It goes without saying that we should be contemporary and consider the latest findings in our daily work.

And here is the bridge to the book by Daniel Memmert and Stefan Leiner. It is precisely this kind of communication of scientific findings, in this case coming from the cognitive sciences, that is helpful for us trainers. Well-founded statements based on research and studies are important. Because let's speak frankly: Who of us is not also stuck in unquestioned training routines or shies away from discussions with athletes about new methods and fears failure with them?

And since we trainers often work in teams where science doesn't really have a voice, where there is little to no exchange between theory and practice, the old routines remain. But we have to move with the times and have the courage to experiment more. To try things out, to refine them, to discard them, and to look at them anew. Science itself does nothing else. This is how quality develops in the training process.

Daniel Memmert and Stefan Leiner first introduce the topic. They make it very clear how important it is to understand and consider the processes in the mind, the cognitive processes, and their high relevance for successful performance and the development of game intelligence in sports. What models and evidence are there on this? The call to coaches is clear: we need to start training cognitive skills systematically in practice.

Furthermore, they present a process model they developed, which describes the central cognitive performance factors. These underlie our actions and attempted solutions in the various match situations.

- How does a given situation in a tennis match actually lead to a solution?

- What phases does the mind go through in any given situation?

The more understanding we gain of this process, the more effectively we can influence it. We can better recognize strengths and weaknesses in an athlete, make them understandable to him, and improve, stabilize, and develop them specifically through supportive forms of training. Terms like *anticipation, perception, attention, creativity,* and *game intelligence* appear here. And since these terms are part of the daily vocabulary in the training process, it is easy to dock here and get involved with the findings, which are presented in an interesting and understandable way.

In this way, game situations may also appear in front of the inner eye. Our perception in our work with our athletes is given more depth and explanation, so to speak. This is helpful for ourselves and for the argumentation situation in the communication with our athletes.

Daniel Memmert and Stefan Leiner present diagnostic tools that can help identify strengths and potential for improvement in our athletes. They transfer the findings into a detailed practical section. Here every trainer will find what he is looking for. Training monotony can be broken. In addition to the forms of exercise presented, one's creativity can be given free rein. Once the principles are understood, there are many more exercise variations that can be developed experimentally.

Cognition is a key performance factor if we want to succeed in sports. This is made crystal clear in this book. I have seen this in top tennis for 30 years. The top players have better-developed skills here. This book combines the latest scientific findings with tools that can be put into practice to specifically improve the cognitive skills that are so important. The exercise forms can be used regardless of age and are transferable to any level of play.

It can help us to integrate new aspects into the training, to question old routines, and to establish ourselves as trainers who are up to date and work according to the latest scientific findings and methods.

If all this is conveyed in an atmosphere of humor, lightness, and openness, the probability of success will increase considerably. We will only find new, more effective ways and approaches if we try them out. Only courage to do so! Let us anchor ourselves in current, scientific knowledge and act more and more from a comprehensive, integral consciousness. That is what I wish for all of us. The book is a beautiful contribution to this.

–Carsten Arriens

**Former Davis Cup team captain, Germany; current coach of Jan-Lennard Struff**

# ACKNOWLEDGEMENTS

We would like to thank numerous colleagues with whom we have had the privilege of researching and publishing on the topic of cognition in recent years and whose ideas we have integrated (alphabetically): Dr. Philip Furley, Prof. Dr. Norbert Hagemann, Jun. Prof. Dr. Stefanie Klatt, Dr. Timo Klein-Soetebier, Prof. Dr. Stefan König, Dr. Benjamin Noël, Prof. Dr. Klaus Roth, Dr. Sebastian Schwab, and Prof. Dr. Matthias Weigelt. Of course, also to all students who made valuable contributions to the individual sub-studies.

A research program rarely results from the ideas of one individual, but rather from the collective thoughts of many in a pleasant atmosphere. In addition, we would like to thank all those who critically proofread parts of the book in advance. These are in particular (alphabetically) Prof. Dr. Norbert Hagemann, Prof. Dr. Oliver Höner, Prof. Dr. Stefan König, Dr. Carina Kreitz, and Prof. Dr. Matthias Weigelt. We would like to express our sincere thanks to Fabian Wunderlich, Erika Graf, Caro Tisson, Conor Cleary, and Sophia Ebner for their assistance in the preparation of the figures and the diverse feedback.

Alexander Satschko (best ATP ranking in singles 259th place; former Bundesliga player, for example for TC Amberg am Schanzl, SV Wacker Burghausen, STC Solingen; current coach of Peter Gojowczyk and Daniel Brands; B-Trainer Leistungssport DTB), Lukas Ollert (best ATP ranking in singles 655th place; currently player in the Second Tennis Bundesliga at TC Iserlohn; cooperation with ATP player Tobias Simon; B-Trainer Leistungssport DTB; RPT International Professional Tennis Director), Maxi Wimmer (current Bundesliga coach of TC Großhesselohe; ATP Tour Coach of e. g. B. Matthias Bachinger, Peter Gojowczyk, Tim Pütz, Christopher Kas, Frank Moser; NCAA coaching license) as well as Frederic

Arlt (Master of Science Diagnostics and Training at the Technical University of Munich; cooperation with ATP player Daniel Brands; Athletic trainer in professional and junior soccer at FC Ingolstadt; B-Trainer Leistungssport DTB; Talentino Scout des Bezirks Niederbayern) have given us a variety of specific ideas and suggestions for the game forms in the practice area, for which we are very grateful.

Dr. Philip Furley has guided us throughout the process, which we greatly appreciate. The many critical comments have been very good for the book and the research work in this area at our institute.

# 1 TENNIS MATCHES ARE DECIDED IN THE HEAD

Roger Federer can find extraordinary—technically and tactically—optimal solutions in highly complex situations. For successful coaches or players, mental speed is important. The head is essential, and to be an exceptional player is to be very quick minded, or game intelligent.

## Statements From Tennis

"You can't play tennis well without being a good thinker. You win or lose the game before you even go out there." –Venus Williams

"Tennis is a mental sport. Everyone is fit, everyone hits good forehands and backhands." –Novak Djokovic

"The skiers fight against the clock. The swimmers fight side by side. Pole vaulters fight one after the other. Footballers fight in packs. Boxers fight toe to toe. Only tennis players duel at a distance. And they are the only ones without a time limit! And until the last minute, it remains uncertain who will be the winner. The decisive qualities for such a duel are strength, diplomacy, concentration, speed, economy, precision, intuition, wit, calmness, self-control, and intellect. And he who does not possess one or the other of these abilities must strive to replace it with the last: intellect." –Erich Kästner (writer)

## Statements From Soccer

"As far as physical presence is concerned, soccer is reaching its limits. In the cognitive field, on the opposite, there are infinite possibilities. A chess player thinks ten to twenty steps ahead; a soccer player should be able to do the same in the future. Some players already can. Özil, Kroos, or Pirlo can play the ball into the depths. They know that one of their teammates will run into it. Such players think one step ahead. So, there is potential to think ahead. That is why I still see great resources in cognitive training. From my point of view, data or statistics about ball possessions are not necessary anymore." –Joachim Löw (German National Coach)

"The Spanish cannot be beaten with tactical aggressiveness, duel strength, or hardness. They cannot be reached with these strategies. They are mentally too fast. And that is exactly what will become an important challenge and development for all players. It is a matter of being mentally fast nowadays. Maybe mental speed is still to be ranked above physical speed. If a player has a good technique and a

good basic speed but is too slow in the head, it can reduce his value to the team."
–Joachim Löw (German National Coach)

"Soccer is about the intelligent play when possessing the ball, about technique in the movement with the ball, and about speed. But I am not only talking about gear. Usain Bolt is fast, but he cannot play soccer. What I mean is mental speed. Soccer is about conquering the ball. As a coach, it is good to have intelligent players who can also play on both feet." –Lucien Favre (German Bundesliga Coach)

In tennis magazines, it is sometimes called action speed, and in tennis books, it is underlined several times that "tennis games are decided in the head" (Memmert et al., 2013). In addition, a large number of studies described in sports science journals confirm the particular importance of linking perceptive abilities and reaction or action speed (known as reactive agility).

**Action speed definition** (Friedrich, 2005, p. 143)

"Especially in sports games, it is essential to implement technical and tactical actions successfully according to the situation. The level of action speed is defined by the total time required for the cognitive processes (mental speed) and the motor solution of the active task."

All concepts and approaches in sports seem to have something in common. The head, and therefore cognition, seems to play a fundamental role during games, and this is particularly evident in soccer.

In sports, cognition is the problem-solving process necessary for generating adequate solutions in specific situations. To this end, this book presents a model of the processes of human decision-making. Cognitive abilities such as anticipation, perception, memory, or attention that contribute to creativity are described. This also includes game intelligence, which describes the selection of the best decision. In a more general sense, cognition can also add will, moods, and emotions. In training, it can now be a matter of practicing all these abilities individually or in combination, making them available in the memory.

Tennis plays a vital role in sports science. There are many research findings on this topic from different disciplines (Edel, Song, Wiewelhove & Ferrauti, 2019; Fernández-García, Blanca-Torres, Nikolaidis & Torres-Luque, 2019; Lees, 2019; Meffert, O'Shannessy, Born, Grambow & Vogt, 2019; Myers et al., 2019; Söğüt, Luz, Kaya & Altunsoy, 2019), especially in the areas of attention, perception, and anticipation, but also regarding creativity and play intelligence as well as working memory. Nevertheless, many scientific results have not yet been transferred into practice.

For the first time, scientifically founded statements about cognitive training in tennis are provided in this book. The content, methods, diagnostics, and practical aspects of the cognitive training are also discussed.

The first part of the book presents the basics of cognitive training: What are the key factors that can be trained? What kinds of models are available? What evidence is available? In addition, these findings are linked to coaching practice. With a single word, coaches can vary the players' focus of attention. Maximum attention is needed in situations where variability and creativity are required. If, on the other hand, movements and actions are to be anticipated, or attention is required for specific events, then a narrow focus of awareness can help. Over the past 15 years, many studies have been conducted, and the role of the working memory in such situations is now apparent.

The possible cognitive diagnostics are subdivided into tests on elementary cognitions in the laboratory or the field on the underlying model. To determine, for example, how significant the attention focus of a player is, his attention window can accurately be determined in the laboratory. In very extensive sport scientific studies with top athletes, there are also attention tests that were developed to precisely specify the attention window of an athlete. In addition, there are also diagnostic tools that can be used in practice. It is possible to see, for example, how players can shield themselves from interfering variables, how distributed or selected their attention is, and how well they are able to focus. There are now numerous test procedures to assess these situations. At the same time, there are established game-related tests in the field (indoor or outdoor) that can be used to evaluate the athletes' skills in finding gaps and releasing in space. These form a basic tactical foundation and are important—not only in tennis, but also in other sports games.

In chapter 5, some cognitive coaching examples are presented. Attention and creativity can be trained. Anticipation particularly, as well as perception and focus, can be excellently trained. In the following chapters, numerous types of games, structured according to the content model of cognitive training, are presented.

# 2 DEFINITION AND RELEVANCE OF COGNITIONS

What exactly is cognition, or cognitive processes, from a scientific perspective?

The use of the term *cognition* has a long tradition, ranging from Tolman to Hebb and Neisser to Gazzaniga—all famous scientists. At this point, no precise overview of the existing diversity of definitions is presented (e.g., for an overview in psychology, Neisser, 2014; for an overview in sport, Memmert, 2004a). In contrast to purely physiological, neuronal, and precognitive processes, Roth and Menzel (2001, p. 539) characterize mental performance through six cognitive processes:

1.  Integrative—often multisensory and experience-based—processes of perception

2.  Processes that involve recognizing individual events and categorizing or classifying objects, people, and events

3.  Processes that take place either consciously or unconsciously based on internal representations (models, imaginations, maps, hypotheses)

4.  Processes that involve an experience-controlled change in perception, thereby leading to changeable processing strategies

5.  Processes that require or include attention, expectations, and active exploration of the stimulus situation

6.  Mental activities

In general, cognition is simply defined as those higher mental functions and processes necessary to generate appropriate solutions in certain situations, in given environments.

The significance of cognitive abilities in sport is not conclusively clarified and is currently the subject of an intensive discussion. This also extends to psychology (for an overview see Simons, et al. 2016; Hambrick, Burgoyne, & Oswald, 2019). Thus, we are currently in an exciting period in sports science and training. While, for example, one working group has been submitting data for years that shows that working memory capacity training is positively related to a different cognitive performance (cf. Klingberg, 2010), another working group was unable to confirm these correlations consistently (cf. Owen, et al., 2010). In theory, it is always a question of whether the training of an elementary cognitive ability leads to transfer effects on other domain-specific performances.

### Executive Functions

An actual model for cognition from psychology (Alvarez & Emory, 2006), which is also occasionally used in sports psychology as a basis for research programs, describes the control and regulation of specific cognitive processes in humans. These executive functions (EF) regulate goal-oriented, future-oriented behavior (Friedman, 2006) (i.e., processes such as decision-making) EF are further divided into core EF (CEF) and higher-level EF (HEF). CEF is formerly characterized by working memory, cognitive flexibility, and inhibitory processes, while HEF involves problem-solving and argumentation strategies, as well as planning processes (Diamond, 2013).

These abilities develop with age as they depend on different prefrontal brain structures. The neuronal structure underlying the HEFs is the prefrontal cortex. It matures slowly and lasts in development; full capacity is reached between 20 and 29 years (Luciana, 2005). CEFs, on the other hand, develop earlier in life, mostly before early adolescence (Crone, 2006). In this book, both form the basis of the models and findings presented. The CEFs are associated with working memory, tracking of objects, inhibition processes using the perception capacities, and flexibility of the attention window, since these develop earlier than the HEFs and thus could be a key indicator in the early development process of players. The HEFs address anticipation, game intelligence, and game creativity, which can also be profitably trained in later training phases.

In two sports science meta-analyses (Voss, et al., 2010; Scharfen & Memmert, 2019a), small to medium effects of essential cognitive performance in experts could be demonstrated, which indicates superior (basal) cognitive abilities of elite athletes. Individual working groups have also discovered that sports experts (especially professional soccer players) seem to possess outstanding basal cognitive skills (Vestberg et al., 2012; Verburgh et al., 2016). However, the number of studies is still too small, the methodological quality is manageable, and there are also some published studies that have not proven any connections (cf. Furley, Schul, & Memmert, 2017).

Finally, a cross-sectional study by Scharfen and Memmert (2019b) of highly talented young soccer players demonstrates that, for example, a significant attention window can be advantageous for more complex motor skills, such as dribbling. In addition, a lower reduction in individual perceptual load indicates a higher sprint speed, and a better working memory affects more precise ball control and dribbling ability. These findings will soon need to be replicated, particularly in larger samples.

A systematic overview of commercial cognitive training programs and their impact on sport practices (Harris, Wilson, & Vine, 2018) shows that many questions remain unanswered and need to be clarified in follow-up studies. Nevertheless, we firmly believe that we must begin to train cognitive skills in practice even before science has answered all of the questions from A to Z. In many places, a little courage is needed, and in other places, humility and restraint is required. The dilemma of general, unspecific domain cognition can be illustrated best by the metaphor of a transport vehicle such as a car or an aircraft.

On the one hand, regardless of whether the vehicle is a sports car, tractor, or truck, the larger the engine (unspecific, since motors are also used in many machines), the faster you will drive. The better the technology (even non-specific), the safer you will be on the road. On the other hand, different means of transport also have different requirement profiles. For example, an aircraft needs different tires and an entirely different engine. However, in the space or automotive industry, the mixture of rubber materials that should be used for the tires of airplanes or cars is already known and perfected, but this cannot yet be said for cognitive processes in complex sports.

### Cognition in Analogy to Lactate

A good endurance (illustrated by the metabolic degradation product lactate) counteracts early fatigue, regardless of the type of sport (e.g., handball, athletics, weight training). This can be demonstrated, for example, in a reduced period of time for recovery between training sessions or between training sets.

In a classic study by Spencer and Gastin (2001), it was possible to prove that even in the 200-meter sprint, which is well under 30 seconds, there is still participation of almost 30% of an aerobic metabolism. Thus, lactate can be described as an unspecific (independent of movement/sport) parameter (analogous to unspecific memory and attention processes) for the aerobic running performance of an athlete.

When lactate was first investigated in soccer 40 years ago (Ekblom, 1986), many were skeptical about its science and practice. Today, lactate diagnostics is an integral part of training control, and its targeted and systematic use has become indispensable in youth and professional soccer.

If we transfer the example of the engine to a sport, this means that an excellent tennis player can benefit from both a broad focus of attention and a large working memory, which can be acquired through a talent selection process or a lot of experience in tennis situations. This brings such an excellent tennis player to the position of making more efficient decisions since he can integrate more players and opponents into the decision-making process.

On the other hand, it is also reasonable that excellent soccer players only score well in attention, working memory, and field performance tests (including talent selection processes), because they have other talents or abilities that influence their gaming performance to a very high degree. For example, this could be high ambition, high motivation, or a high willingness to make an effort.

It is difficult to estimate which of the two positions will provide empirical support in the future. Perhaps both will have their justification, and the *truth* will be in between. For this reason, it is recommended to simultaneously be courageous and humble. In the following chapters, further findings from movement science and sports psychology on elementary cognitions are discussed. And: This is not so little.

# 3 COGNITIONS IN TENNIS

As it applies to sports (e.g., tennis), table 1 shows elementary cognition from a biopsychological, evolutionary, developmental, and cognitive perspective, which can loosely be linked to necessary tactical competences, and, in turn, be of fundamental importance in various sports.

*Table 1: Presentation of elementary cognition with regard to various sub-disciplines that could serve as a cognitive basis for mastering basic tactical tasks in sports games (from Memmert, 2004 a, p. 137)*

| Tasks | Operatio-nalization | Biopsychology | Evolution Psychology | Development Psychology | Cognitive Sciences |
|---|---|---|---|---|---|
| Attacking the goal | Head for time and location | Targeted orientation performance | | Object search | Orientation towards a target |
| Moving ball to goal | Distance estimation | Assessments of directions | | Distance coding | Distance differentiation |
| Using gaps | Spatial decision | Localization of objects | | Object-related perception | Object differentiation |
| Feinting | Ball avoidance | Stimulus-related reactions | Stimulus-related reactions | Concrete reactions | Stimulus-related reactions |
| Interplay | Adequate pass | Temporal-spatial structure of sensations | Object relation | | Visual location/ orientation |
| Creating a majority | Outplay | Spatial imagination | Spatial reactions | Locations reactions | Location reactions |
| Offering and orienting | Spatial orientation | Cognitive Maps | Spatial orien-tation | Spatial cognition | Spatial cognition |

In addition to such basal cognition as using *gaps* (see diagnostics chapter), more complex cognitive abilities have also been discussed in sports science for many years. Based on the paradigms of psychology, a process model of the course of human decision-making was developed (Memmert, 2013, 2017a,b; Memmert & Roth 2003; Roth & Hossner 1999), which includes cognitive abilities such as anticipation, perception, attention, creativity, game intelligence, and memory (see figure 1). This model was primarily developed for games since creativity or attention in swimming or track and field are not as central as they are in soccer. In games, many different possible solutions are needed to succeed.

Tennis players, in particular, want to anticipate a situation based on previous experiences stored in their memory, so individual environmental factors are perceived and considered either consciously or unconsciously. After players have consciously or often unconsciously generated a certain number of solutions in their mind – though only as many as can be retained in their memory – they select a creative idea or the best resolution. This can be illustrated by the following sequence from the semi-final match of Roger Federer vs. Novak Djokovic at the 2016 Australian Open.

**A Practical Example of Cognitions in World-Class Tennis**
(see https://youtu.be/4FqOdvvsEYc)

Roger Federer decides to surprise Djokovic and thus creatively (statistically rare) plays a serve and volley on his backhand. In the run-up, he perceives that, despite his good serve, the return will be played flat, as a slice, back to his feet.

Federer responds intelligently with a half-volley stop, which Djokovic anticipates and then intelligently returns a lob over Federer.

Federer has Djokovic's expected next position in his working memory and plays a lob back.

Djokovic does not manage to win the rally on the offensive, because Federer respectively anticipates the right corner on the defensive. In the end Federer wins the rally with a very creative and surprising backhand passing shot.

He succeeds in deceiving Djokovic, who then covers the wrong side of the net (anticipates incorrectly).

Federer probably has a large attention window, which, in addition to his technical-tactical skills and abilities, enables him to come up with creative and intelligent solutions as in the example video.

In the following, the cognitive factors anticipation, perception, attention, game intelligence, creativity, and memory processes responsible for the successful solution of tactical situations in tennis are accentuated (figure 1). The representation of the individual psychological processes follows a widely accepted temporal sequence, whereby not all perceptive cognitive phases necessarily have to be passed through in the real context.

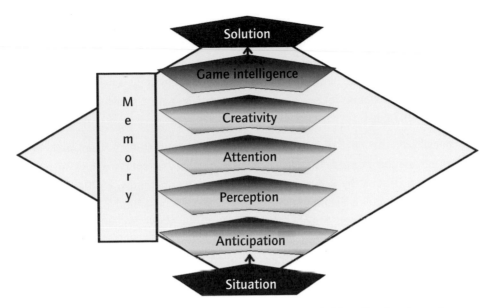

*Figure 1: Overview of the central cognitive performance factors underlying all actions in tennis (Memmert, 2013). All perceptive cognitive phases do not necessarily have to be passed through in order to generate tennis-specific situation solutions.*

# 3.1 Anticipation

Anticipation is significant in many sports games (Hagemann & Loffing, 2013). In tennis, the time to return a first hard serve is so short that returners must anticipate the direction of the ball before contact with the ball or at contact with the ball. For this reason, research in games has dealt with the corresponding latent or obvious indications of the players (e.g., shooter or goalkeeper) in a differentiated way, which can be used to anticipate the intentions of the opposing athletes (cf. in summary Loffing, Cañal-Bruland, & Hagemann, 2014).

Various experiments have confirmed that experts can make earlier and more precise predictions based on the previous direction of movement of the opponents (for good overviews: Williams & Ward, 2003; Farrow & Abernethy, 2007; Loffing, Cañal-Bruland, & Hagemann, 2014). Further studies show that different parts of the body can be classified as information-rich areas (Magill, 1998) and then used to derive clues for subsequent actions (for an overview, Cauraugh, & Janelle, 2002).

## Anticipation in Another Backstroke Sport

In badminton, for example, not only areas distant from the body, such as the racket or the trajectory of the birdie but also the arm and upper body serve as important sources of information for anticipating the opponent's next stroke (Abernethy & Russell, 1987a, b).

Especially in the field of backstroke sports, numerous studies have analyzed the anticipation process. They have covered a variety of sports games such as badminton (Abernethy & Russell, 1987a, b); squash (Abernethy, 1990a; 1990b); table tennis (Ripoll & Fleurance, 1988); and tennis (Goulet, Bard & Fleury, 1989; Singer, Cauraugh, Chen, Steinberg & Frehlich, 1996; Ward, Williams & Bennett, 2002). Anticipatory skills acquired in this way can be partially transferred to later performance in real competitive situations (cf. Farrow & Abernethy, 2002; Williams, Ward & Chapman, 2003).

In tennis, only groundstrokes and serves have been used to study anticipatory abilities, and consistently found that tennis experts can anticipate more accurately than tennis novices (e.g., Triolet, Benguigui, Le Runigo & Williams, 2013; Smeeton & Huys, 2011). On the other hand, it is surprising that anticipatory behavior in real-world play can be observed almost exclusively in situations where the opponent has a significant tactical advantage (Triolet, Benguigui, Le Runigo & Williams, 2013).

The classic study of tennis by Williams, Ward, Knowles, and Smeeton (2002) was able to show (see figure 2) that less skilled players prefer to focus on the racket and ball regions of the server. In contrast, experts use a more synthetic search strategy, using prior knowledge and experience to direct their gaze to additional, perhaps more subtle, task-relevant information sites located around the central body regions (e.g., head-shoulder, trunk-hip). Players who received perceptual training, relative to these findings, improved their anticipation performance on the return, both in the laboratory and in the field, compared to placebo and control groups who did not receive such instruction.

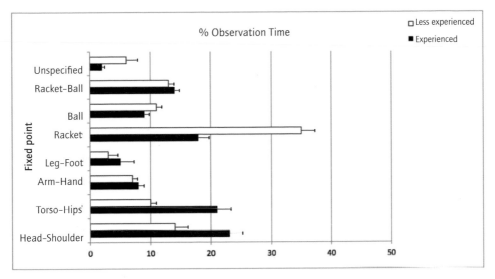

*Figure 2: Anticipation-relevant regions in the tennis serve for the return player identified by less experienced and experienced players (from Williams et al., 2002).*

The findings of Williams et al. (2002) were confirmed by Jackson and Mogan (2010). In tennis serving, the results indicate that information from the ball toss and the arm and racket region improves anticipation performance and that more expertise is associated with an increasing awareness of the information on which judgments are based.

Although Huys et al. (2009) observed a decrease in anticipation performance when local information from arm/racket as well as trunk/legs was masked, the results generally suggest that successful tennis players can anticipate stroke direction by using a more global perceptual approach, especially for top players.

Another important clue seems to be to disguise one's rackets, Rowe, Horswill, Kronvall-Parkinson, Poulter, and McKenna (2009) showed that disguising significantly reduces the accuracy of anticipation. The anticipatory advantage of experts is eliminated by obfuscation at 40 ms before bat-ball contact. These results suggest that concealment is an important topic for research and practice.

Numerous studies have also addressed training anticipation in games (for a good overview, Loffing, Hagemann, & Farrow, 2017). In general, sport-specific anticipation information is taught via film-based simulations or through rare on-site training sessions using a live model (badminton: Tayler, Burwitz, & Davids, 1994; field hockey: Williams, Ward & Chapman, 2003; soccer: Savelsbergh, van Gastel, & van Kampen, 2010; squash: Abernethy, Wood, & Parks, 1999). These results can be used to design training programs in order to test whether they can improve the anticipation skills of athletes, especially beginners.

A particularly relevant question is how anticipation skills can be promoted by different teaching methods (see Farrow & Abernethy, 2002; Smeeton, Williams, Hodges & North, 2004; Williams, Ward & Chapman, 2003; Williams, Ward, Knowles & Smeeton, 2002). Which form of instruction is the most promising to facilitate the learning of anticipatory skills?

Memmert et al. (2009) tested various training conditions (principle from *simple* to *complex*, context interference conditions, and feedback effects) for the improvement of anticipation skills. It has been shown that variable, randomized training with little feedback is advantageous. Other studies have evaluated explicit, implicit, and controlled explorative learning. Jackson and Farrow (2002) present an overview of the different approaches to the training of anticipatory skills, and discuss the possible benefits of implicit learning methods.

In addition, it could be demonstrated that a sport-specific anticipation ability can be developed without requiring a direct connection between perception and motor skills (sport-specific movement technique) (Williams, Ward, Smeeton, & Allen, 2004). This enables perception training under laboratory conditions for injured athletes, athletes who are on their way to competition, or athletes who would like additional practice at home. Hagemann and Memmert (2006) also showed that verbal instructions and appropriate badminton tasks within a real field-based training program improved anticipation performance just as much as a video-based laboratory program.

**Example: Effectiveness of Anticipation Training in the Field**

A training study by Hagemann and Memmert (2006) will be used as an example to illustrate that field-based anticipation training can also lead to an improvement in specific anticipation abilities, compared to laboratory-based anticipation training (using video clips). The field-based training intervention was based on findings of the anticipation ability in badminton (Abernethy & Russell, 1987). All players were given tasks to predict the direction of an opponent's shot. The anticipation performance was recorded before and after the intervention, and in a later transfer test, with an established badminton-specific anticipation test (Abernethy & Russell, 1987). The results of the field-based intervention show that it is possible to train the anticipation of overhead strokes in badminton. This is unaffected by the trainer and was confirmed by the fact that all participants of the various training groups, at two different universities (Heidelberg and Münster), improved their anticipatory performance. The reason for why anticipation skills of the field-based intervention are slightly reduced, compared to those of the laboratory-based intervention, may be due to most players being beginners since the exercises were usually performed with a partner from the same training group. The analysis of the video clips with regard to the expertise of the test persons explicitly shows this. The participants in the laboratory-based intervention, the only group to receive video material with Bundesliga players, usually show a successful adaptation by anticipating the strokes of Bundesliga players, but not those of novices or regional league players. This confirms the importance of using experts as role models in the training process, especially considering that it is generally more difficult to predict the direction of Bundesliga players.

The use of instructions thus enables coaches to direct the athletes' attention to anticipation-relevant regions that contain the most essential movement characteristics.

# 3.2 Perception

Perceptual abilities also play a dominant role in sport (Williams, Davids, & Williams, 1999). Sports games are often characterized by complex situations in which appropriate reactions have to be evoked in the shortest possible time. The (correct) perception and use of information is therefore crucial for a successful action planning and execution, which is why outstanding athletes differ from average athletes in this ability.

> Andy Murray immediately recognizes that his opponent is only faking a forehand winner, but in reality, wants to play a drop-shot and can therefore easily run the ball and win the point.
>
> ---
>
> Serena Williams reads the defensive behavior of her opponents particularly well and because of that she often manages to play balls against their running direction.

For example, an athlete has to precisely understand the game situation within a short space of time to be able to react correctly. Interactions with teammates and reactions to pponents are elementary in tennis because without exact information from the environment, it is difficult to plan an appropriate course of action. Various aspects of perception are relevant, such as the position of opponents, free spaces, and distances. Latest research demonstrates that even tactical creativity is underpinned by different underlying perceptual processes (Roca, Memmert, & Ford, 2018; Roca, Ford, & Memmert, 2020).

"Perception is defined as the subjective impression of our environment or our body, shaped by the sensory processing of stimuli from various sensory modalities. Put simply, perception describes the process of receiving, selecting, and processing different stimuli, and forms the basis of human knowledge, experience, and action (Marr, 1982). Individually made experiences are based on information that a person receives through senses, processes, and stores in subcortical and cortical recognition structures of the different perception systems (Bruce, Green, & Georgeson, 1996). Perceptual processes therefore initially include all activities that serve to obtain information. Human perception takes place through one or more senses and helps to grasp and classify the environment. Visual perception plays a very important role in many everyday situations, as well as in sports. It describes the absorption and transmission of various stimuli with the help of the eye—in short, the sense of sight. From a physiological perspective, visual perception involves the absorption of photons using photoreceptors in the eye and the conversion of these stimuli into electrical signals, which are first recorded, processed, and interpreted in the occipital area of the brain and then in many other brain regions. On the psychological level, visual perception represents the recording of colour, form/shapes, or movement. These components represent one of the most important, if not the most important, ways of perceiving one's environment for humans, as various situations are usually interpreted and decisions made on the basis of visual perception." (Memmert, Hüttermann, & Kreitz, 2019)

In the following, various findings (some from tennis, but mainly from soccer), which can be roughly classified into the following four areas, are discussed (see table 2).

*Table 2: Classification of the previous findings on perception training in soccer*

| Information processing of the opponent | Information ability of the athlete (intention to act) | | | |
|---|---|---|---|---|
| | Conscious | Correct | Conscious | Incorrect (deception) |
| | Unconscious | Correct | Unconscious | Incorrect (deception) |

### 3.2.1 Conscious Perception Processes Based on Correct Information

Conscious perceptual processes based on correct information have been the most intensively investigated. Most research approaches determine the perception strategies of sports players on the basis of eye movement analyses (for an overview Hüttermann, Noel, & Memmert, 2018; Kredel, Vater, Klostermann, & Hossner, 2017). In summary, it can be shown that experienced sports players have learned to improve their perceptual performance through targeted strategies (Williams et al. 2010). In an overview article by Mann, Williams, Ward, and Janelle (2007), differences in perception strategies between soccer experts and novices were discussed. The experts used fewer but longer gaze fixations, which are mostly directed at fellow players and opponents (cf. figure 3). Unsurprisingly, experts recognized game sequences more accurately than less experienced athletes (e.g., Goulet, Bard & Fleury, 1989). The results of Shim, Carlton, Chow, and Chae (2010) suggest that tennis experts are able to use motion information during time-critical tennis strokes to determine the direction and use this information to significantly reduce their reaction times.

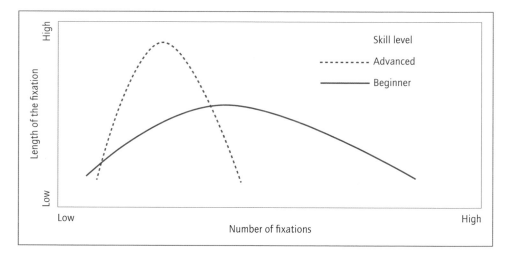

Figure 3: Generalized relationship between number of fixations and duration of fixations (from Tenenbaum, 2003, p. 197).

Numerous studies in soccer have gained insights with the help of eye-tracking (for an overview, Schulz et al., 2018). This shows that excellent soccer players can already deduce the intentions of teammates and opponents before a corresponding action has been carried out. They therefore know that relevant parts of the opponent's body, spots on the court (cf. figure 4), and the point in time information is perceived are all particularly important in their environment (information-rich areas; see figure 2 in Anticipation section), so they keep their gaze on these places longer (see figure 3).

Specifically in tennis, Ward, Williams, and Bennett (2002) demonstrated that experienced tennis players show superior performance in anticipating groundstrokes through their efficient information intake and more selective visual search strategies. This strategy focuses on the relative motion sequences—head/shoulders and trunk/hips (cf. figure 2)—which provide sufficient task-relevant information. Compared to experienced tennis players, inexperienced participants show less consistent visual search strategies across viewing conditions as a consequence of their more exploratory, stimulated gaze behavior (cf. figure 3).

Shim, Carlton, and Kwon (2006) were able to confirm that the racket and forearm in particular provide important *information-rich areas* for anticipating groundstrokes. Shim, Miller, and Lutz (2005) also showed that observing the relative motion between the racket and forearm provides players with the most valuable visual information. The relative motion of the racket and forearm proved to be important not in perceiving the direction of the opponent's stroke, but in perceiving the type of stroke delivered by the opponent (here: forehand down and across and lob to forehand and backhand corner).

In the case of anticipating the serve, the findings of Jackson and Mogan (2010) were able to indicate that information from the ball toss and the arm and bat region underpinned players' anticipation ability and that greater expertise was accompanied by increased awareness of the information on which judgments were based. The ability to anticipate an opponent's serve can also be enhanced by on court instruction that clarifies the relationship between important cues (see figure 2) (Williams, Ward, Smeeton, & Allen 2004).

Trainers can help the players to select and focus on the right sources of information. These information-rich areas can be dependent on one's own previous knowledge (e.g., knowledge of the opponent) (Jackson, Warren, & Abernethy 2006), and increase perception through greater efficiency. Trainers can unintentionally draw attention to unimportant and somewhat irrelevant aspects of the action through their speeches. For example, the sentence "Do not pay attention to the goalkeeper" has the exact opposite effect on most players; the result is a more extended focus on the goalkeeper and more shots aimed in his direction (Bakker, Oudejans, Binsch, & van der Kamp, 2006).

## 3.2.2 Conscious Perception Processes Based on Incorrect Information (Deceptions)

A form of consciously used but *incorrect* perception information is transported by deceptive actions (for an overview, Güldenpenning, Kunde, & Weigelt, 2017): for example, a player tries to fake a forehand shot only to play a drop-shot. To our knowledge, there are no studies on this in tennis.

Within all studies of the field of soccer, it can be demonstrated that deceptions are meaningful and effective. Goalkeepers unsurprisingly hold fewer shots with deception than without (Dicks, Button, & Davids, 2010), and experts are better able to predict shots with deception than novices (Bishop et al. 2013; Smeeton & Williams, 2012). Soccer players also reacted more quickly to deceptions that coincide with the normal direction of the deception than if they did not (Wright & Jackson, 2014). However, the inclusion of early visual information (running, visual, and body deceptions) offers no significant advantage (Bishop et al. 2013) so players are well-advised to concentrate on the player's football contacts. However, visual search patterns show no difference between shots with and without deception (Tay et al., 2012). It should also be mentioned that in soccer, there are more studies from the perspective of the goalkeeper than from the perspective of the field players (Güldenpenning, et al., 2017).

## 3.2.3 Unconscious Perception Processes Based on Correct Information

Environmental stimuli can be perceived both consciously and unconsciously. Today we know from general psychology and motoric research that perception and action influence each other (Prinz, 1997). This could be demonstrated in a series of experiments within the framework of a penalty shoot-out situation (Masters, van der Kamp & Jackson 2007; Weigelt, Memmert & Schack, 2012; Noel et al., 2015). The study shows that even unconsciously perceived information can strongly influence motor actions (see box).

---

**Unconscious Perception Influences Conscious Behavior**

In numerous studies conducted by working groups from Amsterdam, Paderborn, and Cologne, the goalkeeper's position on the goal line at the soccer penalty kick has been used as a study paradigm to support this statement (Weigelt, Memmert & Schack, 2012; Noël, van der Kamp, & Memmert, 2015; Noël, van der Kamp, Weigelt, & Memmert, 2015; Noël, van der Kamp, Masters, & Memmert, 2016; Weigelt, Memmert & Schack, 2012). For this purpose, the goalkeeper was systematically moved slightly more to the left or right of the goal center on the goal line (cf. figure 4).

In fact, there is a high probability that the shooter will shoot to the right if a goalkeeper is placed to the left of the center of the goal from the shooter's point of view. This effect also exists if the goalkeeper position deviates only very slightly from the center and the shooters do not consciously perceive this shift (Noël, van der Kamp, Weigelt, & Memmert, 2015). Both experienced and inexperienced players are equally influenced by the unnoticeable change in position (Weigelt, Memmert & Schack, 2012).

With the knowledge of this connection, goalkeepers could more consciously choose their position on the penalty kick. By placing the goalkeeper on his *weak* goal side—minimally away from the goal center—the probability that the shooters aim at the opposite corner increases. This in turn means that the goalkeeper has a higher chance of keeping the shot on his *strong* goal side.

---

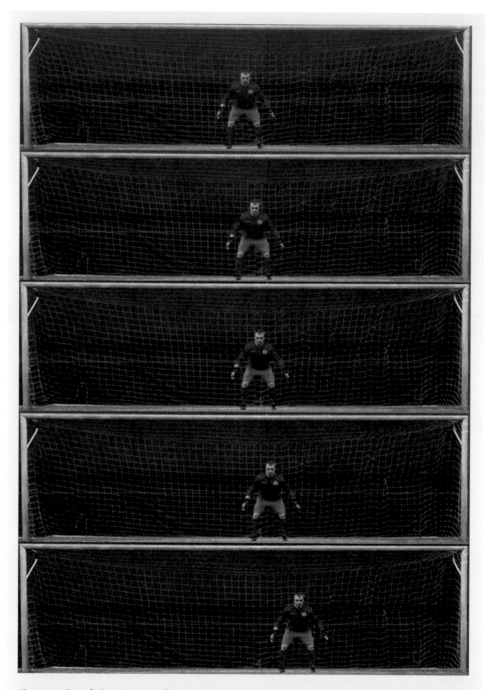

Figure 4: Five of nine pictures of the goalkeeper in a neutral position with the left arm stretched out. The goalkeeper was shown in a neutral goalkeeper position, either in the center of the goal or in one of four displaced positions left (not shown here) or right of the center.

## 3.2.4 Unconscious Perception Processes Based on Incorrect Information (Deceptions)

Surprisingly, there are hardly any research studies that address unconscious processes of perception based on incorrect information (deceptions). Güldenpenning and colleagues argued in first experiments that false information (i.e., incorrect information) could also be processed unconsciously (Güldenpenning, Steinke, Koester, & Schack, 2013; Güldenpenning, Braun, Machlitt, & Schack, 2015). This would make it possible for athletes to implicitly process body-related information through priming (unconsciously perceived information), which in turn can activate motor reactions without being explicitly evaluated. In soccer, individual studies from the Cologne and Paderborn working groups could also be interpreted as examples of unconscious perception processes based on incorrect information if the goalkeeper's shift is made consciously (almost as deception) by the goalkeeper, but is not consciously perceived by the shooter (Noël et al., 2015).

# 3.3 Attention

In the process of evolution, the human brain has been optimized to consciously select and process information from the multitude of information that is relevant for goal-oriented action in everyday life, and also in sport (Cohen, Nakayama, Konkle, Stantic, & Alvarez, 2016; Mack & Rock, 1998).

Although attention and perception are closely linked, they are not identical concepts. For example, the spatial distribution of attention differs from the spatial distribution of visual perception (Intriligator & Cavanagh, 2001). Visual perception provides the input for many other cognitive processes, so differences in visual perception can have far-reaching consequences. However, cognition and performance involve much more than the sensory system, and experienced experts can differ from novices in many ways, even if novices had equally good visual perception.

Attention is regarded as a critical factor for athletic performance (Abernethy et al., 2007; Memmert, 2009; Moran, 1996; Wulf, 2007). Soccer players need adequate attention skills while simultaneously performing various activities in order to be able to act successfully in complex situations, while tennis players need adequate attentional skills in the simultaneous execution of different activities in order to perform successfully in complex situations (Tudos, Predoiu, & Predoiu, 2015). For example, in tennis, players have to keep an eye on the ball and also on the opponent, and tennis umpires have to keep an exact eye on relevant information in order to decide whether to call a ball out or not.

### Example: Offside Decision in Soccer

The offside decision in soccer is the result of a remarkable attention performance of the linesmen. In order to make this decision, they have to keep an eye on the numerous players and ball at the same time, since their moves are relative to each other. However, since they run over an extensive area and the eye needs 130 to 160 milliseconds for a change of view between two objects, a linesman can only perceive most of the actions peripherally. On long passes, where the distance between the ball and the offside candidate is particularly long, the offside situation is difficult to check (Hüttermann, Noël, & Memmert, 2017). It can be assumed that referees with a *large attention window* have an advantage in being able to make correct decisions.

As tennis players are continuously confronted with a multitude of visual and auditory stimuli in the specific situations of their sports, which they cannot adequately process due to limited processing capacity, the question of how attention can effectively be directed in order to make optimal decisions arises. Athletes should be able to direct their attention so that they can select relevant information from the less relevant information. Due to the enormous importance of attention, psychological test methods for measurement have been developed (cf. chapter 4 on diagnostics), as well as different models for optimal attention direction in psychology.

The attention mechanism is often explained by the spotlight metaphor: Attention is a type of spotlight whose beam casts light on a specific area (Posner, 1980). The size of the beam is variable (Eriksen & St. James, 1986) and objects in the center of the funnel can be processed better than information in the periphery (LaBerge, 1983).

Since humans have a limited capacity for attention (Broadbent, 1958; Cowan, 1995), we need to hide or attenuate information from our environment in order to work effectively with behavioral events. For this reason, attention theories, paradigms, and mechanisms have already been considered necessary for a long time, and have been intensively studied in cognitive science for almost 100 years (Styles, 2008).

Neuroscientific and cognitive-psychological findings in attention research (e.g., Coull, 1998; Knudsen, 2007; Mirsky, Anthony, Duncan, Ahearn, & Kellam, 1991; Van Zomeren & Brouwer, 1994) suggest a separation of attention into four sub-processes: attention orientation, selective attention, divided attention, and concentration.

**Definitions of the Four Sub-Processes of Attention** (Memmert & Furley, 2012)

- **Attention orientation:** Log in and log out the attention for a certain stimulus.

- **Selective attention:** Select between competing stimuli at a given time.

- **Divided attention:** Simultaneously distribute attention to different stimuli (multitasking).

- **Concentration:** Maintain attention to a specific stimulus over a period of time.

Two of the four sub-processes of attention are further described in more detail in figure 6 to make the attention services relevant in the world of sport more comprehensible and trainable. The focus is on selective and divided attention because these two play a central role in many sports games. The sub-processes of attention orientation and concentration can be found in detail in a separate section (Memmert, 2009).

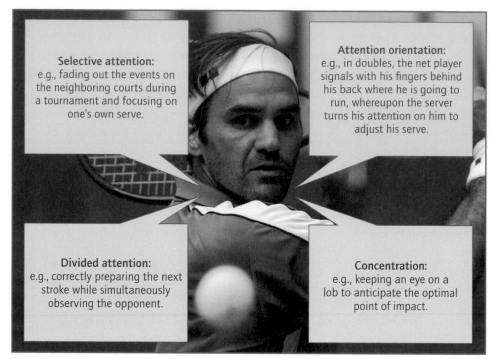

*Figure 5: Presentation of the four sub-processes of attention based on practical examples (attention orientation, selective attention, divided attention, and concentration) using the example of soccer-specific requirements (Furley & Memmert, 2009).*

## 3.3.1 Selective Attention

The sub-process of selective attention allows a targeted spatial or object-related focus at particular moments in time or within specific periods. While the focus is deliberately on certain events, others are inhibited (i.e., excluded) (Coull, 1998; Posner & Boies, 1971).

Selective attention is closely linked to attention orientation because both of these sub-processes are involved in the direction of attention. However, Posner and Peterson (1990) were able to prove that the two attention processes activate different brain areas (i.e., have different neurophysiological bases).

Selective attention selects from different stimuli, while orientation then logs in attention to this stimulus.

Selective attention is the most considered and discussed component in sports science. This is not only due to the fact that this attention process is the most important in sports-specific situations, but also because there are various ways of methodically examining selective attention. For example, it has been demonstrated that selective attention focus can be manipulated by simple instructions. A small instruction from a trainer can restrict and guide the attention focus in such a way that important circumstances of a situation (e.g., an uncovered player) are not consciously perceived, and thus cannot be included in the decision-making process (Memmert & Furley, 2007). Creative solution finding is therefore severely limited. In a six-month longitudinal study, these findings could be replicated in real training scenarios; children achieved no learning improvement in the creative solution of tactical tasks if their attention focus was permanently restricted by precise instructions and tips (Memmert, 2007).

## 3.3.2 Divided Attention

In some situations, it is crucial and necessary to selectively focus attention on an object or a place (see section on selective attention). In other situations, it is required to process several pieces of information at different places in parallel. The sub-process of shared attention enables athletes to concentrate on two or more sources of information simultaneously (see Coull, 1998). This ability, which also requires a sufficient range of attention focus, is an important factor not only in sports but also in various everyday situations such as road traffic.

### Internal vs. External Focus of Attention

A large number of studies deal with motor expertise within the framework of the internal vs. external attentional focus paradigm (for an overview, see Wulf, 2007). In the internal, movement-based focus, the learner directs his or her attentional focus directly to the movement (e.g., movement sequence in a tennis serve). In the external, goal-oriented focus, on the other hand, attention is focused on the movement effect or on the movement goal (e.g., a specific area in the tennis serve).

Nearly all findings suggest that an externalist attentional focus is generally superior to an internalist, movement-based focus across many different movement skills, skill levels, and target groups (in tennis, see: Guillot, Desliens, Rouyer & Rogowski, 2013; Hadler, Chiviacowsky, Wulf & Schild, 2014).

An external attentional focus leads to better learning performance not only for novices but also for experts (Wulf, McConnel, Gärtner & Schwarz, 2002; cf. Gray [2004] for a more nuanced position). Beilock and colleagues can further demonstrate that experts in particular are more likely to be disturbed by an internal attentional focus when performing their highly automated movement (Beilock, Carr, MacMahon & Starkes, 2002).

Hüttermann, Memmert, Simons and Bock (2013) developed a new paradigm with which the visual attention window of a person can be precisely determined. This represents the maximum consciously perceptible field of attention in the horizontal, vertical, and diagonal directions. The attention field is distinguishable from the pure peripheral visual performance. On average, a maximum attention window with a horizontal orientation of 32.88° ± 8.36°, a vertical of 26.40° ± 5.36°, and a diagonal of 27.76° ± 5.56° appears. Experts (sports game players) have larger attention windows than novices (non-sports game players), at least in terms of horizontal and diagonal alignment (see figure 6).

Hüttermann, Memmert, Simons, and Bock (2013) were also able to use the attention window paradigm to clarify the question of whether a fixation between two stimuli is more promising than the fixation of one stimulus with the peripheral perception of the other stimulus. The comparison of both alignment strategies of visual attention showed an average higher success rate (90.42% ± 4.88%) in the identification of simultaneously presented stimuli, compared to the combination of fixed/peripheral alignment (80.24% ± 10.28%). This result seems to be valid for both sports game players and non-sports game players. However, experts in sports games are superior to novices in both strategies.

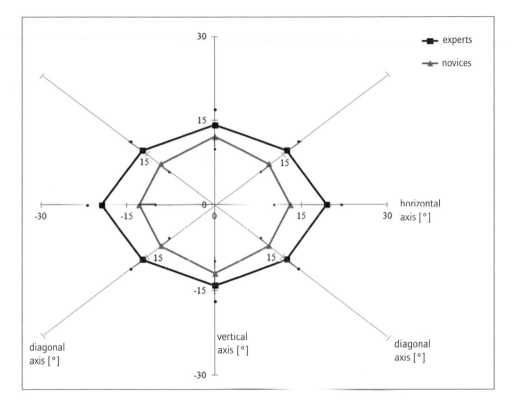

*Figure 6: Size of the maximum attention window (in °) for two different athletes from soccer during which two stimuli can be perceived peripherally simultaneously. Since each pair of stimuli was presented symmetrically across the center, the data is also presented symmetrically for each axis (horizontal, diagonal, vertical). The external attention window displays the averaged values of a Bundesliga player, the interior window the averaged values of a regional league player, and the error bars indicate the respective standard deviations.*

In the phenomenon of inattentional blindness, the basic idea is that when athletes draw their attention to a particular object, they often do not consciously perceive unexpected objects, even though they are directly and clearly visible to their eyes (Mack & Rock, 1998; Most, Scholl, Clifford, & Simons, 2005).

### What Is Inattentional Blindness?

It happens that a player does not see or play towards an utterly free teammate, even though he was clearly in his visual focus. A player persistently claiming not to have seen his teammate quickly creates frustration in coaches and teammates. This player can in fact be right because it is only when attention is directed to a certain area or a particular object that this information is consciously recorded and processed. Conscious perception, therefore, seems to require attention processes. If attention is directed to another object, then an unexpected purpose is often not perceived, even when it may have been in the visual focus of the athlete.

Even high-level youth handball players have not been able to escape this phenomenon (Furley and Memmert, 2007). If their attention was focused on the direct opponent, they no longer saw the free teammate. Basketball experts in the same situation were also not in a position to identify free players who would have represented the optimal solution for the game situation (Furley, Memmert & Heller, 2010). These result patterns were also recognized in more realistic contexts with motor response actions, as well as with a task closer to the field (triple choice task) (see figure 7a). Other scenarios which demanded decision-making tasks and complex attention tasks were also able to confirm these findings (see figure 7b, right).

*Figure 7: Illustration of two sports-specific inattentional blindness test scenarios of different complexity levels: (a) low complexity, handball; 3 vs. 3, Memmert & Furley, 2007; (b) medium complexity, basketball, 5 vs. 5, Furley et al., 2010). The free player, who—according to expert opinion—is also the best solution in this situation, is circled.*

# 3.4 Game Intelligence

For generating possibilities of decisions and finding optimal solutions, a player must be able to perceive all important information from his environment (teammates, opponents, suddenly appearing players, etc.) in order to consider them in his action plan. In soccer, the midfielders in particular have the task of structuring a team's offensive game through smart, rehearsed, tactical behavior. In this context, sports science likes to speak of decision-making ability or, based on psychology, of convergent thinking or (game) intelligence.

> **Definition**
>
> **tactical play intelligence (convergent tactical thinking)**—In team and racket sports, tactical game intelligence means the creation of the best solution to problems in specific individual, group, or team tactical game situations.

The research of sports games mainly works with two definitions of cognitive thinking processes, established by the research group around Joy Paul Guilford: convergent and divergent thinking (Roth, 2005).

In convergent thinking processes, ideal problem solutions are sought and targeted. Divergent thought processes, on the other hand, generate a multitude of problem solutions, particularly solutions that are new, unexpected, or surprising.

Research on tactical game intelligence is closely linked to cognitive decision research (Höner, 2005; Roth, 2005). In sports, it is often called *tactics*. At this point, it is not possible to give a comprehensive overview of tactics research in sports games or soccer. For this purpose, reference must be made to further studies (for an overview, Memmert, 2004a, b). An actual summary of theories and models can be found in König and Memmert (2019).

In tennis, there are numerous studies examining tennis specific training programs to improve tennis players' tactical knowledge and cognitive skills (Raschke & Lames, 2019, among others). For example, García-González, Moreno, Gil, Moreno, and Del Villar (2014) found significant improvements in performance, including retention tests, during a 10-week decision training program.

Professional tennis players have greater, more sophisticated, and more demanding tactical knowledge. With expertise, more complex structures can be developed in long-term memory (García-González, Iglesias, Moreno, Moreno, & Del Villar, 2012). Based on the expert-novice paradigm, Del Villar, García-González, Iglesias, Moreno, and Cervelló (2007) examine decision-making in serve-and-hit actions in competitive forms of competition. Experts show a greater ability to make the right decisions by choosing the best tactical solution to put pressure on the opponent (see also McPherson & Thomas, 1989).

At this point, the focus is on individual tactical cognitive solutions. This often touches on the construct of (tactical) playing ability (cf. Kuhlmann, 1998; Roth, 2005; see table 3). "The construct of playing ability has undoubtedly become a central guiding idea of game mediation" (König, 1997, p. 209). Thus, the general ability to play sports can be compared with the g-factor in general intelligence research.

As table 3 shows, there are numerous, sometimes even quite different, concepts and systematics, as well as contradictory definitions for the construct of playing ability (for a detailed discussion see König, 1997, p. 476).

Basic tactics play a significant role in the development of general playing ability or game intelligence (cf. Memmert & König, 2013). They can be described as basic tactical knowledge that plays a central role in many sports games (cf. table 4). In the meantime, they have become an integral part of numerous teaching plans and training concepts in various age and performance classes (general ball school: Kröger & Roth, 1999; Roth & Kröger, 2011; ball school racket games: Roth, Kröger & Memmert, 2002; ball school throwing games: Roth, Memmert & Schubert, 2006; Soccer: Memmert, Thumfart, & Uhing, 2014).

*Table 3: Definitions of the construct of playing ability in sports games (from Memmert, 2004a, p. 241)*

| Labelling | Definition | Operatio-nalization | Author |
|---|---|---|---|
| Game intelligence/tactical flexibility | The ability to find the right decisions quickly in changed, unforeseen situations, and to find solutions in a tactically useful way. | – | Döbler (1964) |
| Athletic playing activity | Diverse and complex appearance, whose quality is determined by numerous performance factors.<br><br>From a psychological point of view, it can be seen as a unit of motivational, volitive, emotional, and cognitive processes, which find their manifestation in the sport's game-specific motor function. Characteristic of this is the multiple reference system—player, opponent, ball, target area—in which the player is located and with which he must constantly actively interact. | – | Konzag & Konzag (1980) |
| General and special playing ability | The ability to initiate a game, back it up as it progresses, and re-establish it in the case of disturbances.<br><br>The existence of knowledge about the game idea and rules, the necessary skills in handling the game equipment, and tactical experience in important game situations. | – | Dietrich (1984) |
| Playing activity | Targeted conscious tactical maneuvers.<br><br>Tactical knowledge is the basis for the perception and analysis of the game situation and for the game performance. | – | Herzog (1986) |
| Playing ability | The complex ability to solve the various and constantly changing game situations even under opponent interference. | – | Stiehler, Konzag, & Döbler (1988) |
| Playing ability | Complex game-specific performance requirements and a form of individual ability to act according to the variable competition conditions. | – | Schnabel & Thiess (1993) |
| Tactical action | The appropriate and effective coping of complex game situations. | X | Wegner & Katzenberger (1994) |
| Playing ability | The ability to participate actively and successfully in a sports game as a teammate and opponent by coping with typical game situations and game processes within the framework of the rules, technically and tactically, individually or in teamwork with others, by experiencing and shaping the game emotionally. | – | König (1997) |

*Table 4: Basic tactics in racquet games (Roth, Kroger & Memmert, 2002)*

- **Play Out a Superior Number:** Tactical tasks in which it is important to gain an advantage by offering, orienting, and cooperating with partners.

- **Go to the Goal:** Tactical tasks in which it is important to choose the time and place of the final action.

- **Exploit the Gaps:** Tactical tasks in which it is important to (individually) use gaps for the chance of a clearance or point win in the confrontation with opponents.

- **Interplay:** Tactical tasks in which it is important to pass the balls to partners quickly and according to the situation.

- **Approaching the Ball to the Target:** Tactical tasks in which it is important to transport the ball into an attacking or finishing area.

The primary tactics in table 4 can be used as a first starting point for tactical game types, which can help to train tactical game intelligence in training, in talent development, and in the preparation of beginners in school (educational plans for playing ability).

# 3.5 Game Creativity

If you ask tennis experts or take a close look at top international tennis, you can see that it's the highly creative athletes who can make the difference. Pierre Paganini, fitness coach to Roger Federer and Stan Wawrinka, has an explanation for Federer's success, namely that his personality controls him within. He is an artist who is impressively creative and allows his strong emotion to flow into the game.

In addition to tactical game intelligence, another cognitive thinking process plays a significant role in the team and racket sports games: tactical creativity.

In soccer this is no different. When Lionel Messi was named World Player of the Year for the third time, it was said that he "plays on a totally different level" (Neymar da Silva Santos Júnior). Frank Ribery was voted Player of the Year in Europe in 2013; "Besides Ribéry, we have one more player that brings that kind of creativity into the game in minimal space. We want to improve. This can be possible only with extraordinary players," (Louis Van

Gaal about Arjen Robben). Arjen Robben scored the winning goal in the Champions League Final 2013; "he makes the difference; he brings the unpredictability in the game and takes the team with him" (Franz Beckenbauer about Arjen Robben).

---

**Definition**

**tactical creativity (divergent tactical thinking)**—In team and racket sports, tactical creativity is the generation of numerous solutions to problems in specific individual, group, or team tactical game situations that can be described as surprising, rare, and/or original.

---

Creativity in tennis means particularly surprising, original, and flexible tactical and motor solutions such as rhythm changes through drop-shot or angle balls, cut changes, unexpected net attacks, or even lobs to get out of defensive situations. The first empirical findings on the importance of tactical creativity in professional soccer were published in a recent study by Kempe and Memmert (2018).

### Is Creativity a Strong Element in Professional Soccer?

Memmert and Kempe (2018) have examined all matches of the 2010 and 2014 World Cups and the 2016 European Championship in soccer for creative actions in scoring goals. All goals that emerged from the game were analyzed, which totaled 311 goals in 153 games. In each case, the game situations and actions that resulted in a goal were evaluated. The last eight actions that resulted in the goal were included. Three soccer experts with UEFA licenses had the task of rating the actions before the goal in terms of creative performance, on a scale from 1 to 10 with 1 representing a significantly below-average level of creativity and 10 a significantly above-average level of creativity.

The results show that as the level of creativity increases, the closer the actions get to the goal. The seventh action, in particular, the decisive pass (assist), received the highest average level of creativity. Overall, the last three actions before the goal shot had significantly higher creativity values than the actions before. Even if these values are only slightly above the average, this shows that highly creative solutions are extremely rare. The experts rated only 172 out of over 1,800 actions as highly creative, with a score of 8 or higher on the creativity scale.

On the other hand, in almost half of all goals (46%), the action sequences contained at least one action with a high level of creativity. For the very successful teams of the three tournaments, the figure was even 63%. Memmert and Kempe (2018) were also able to show that creativity distinguishes successful from less successful teams in a tournament. In summary, creativity seems to be an increasingly important factor in soccer, particularly when it comes to scoring goals at the highest level of performance.

In order to be able to evaluate such a broad term as tactical creativity, Guilford's research group operationalized it in 1967, dividing it into three properties: originality, flexibility, and fluidity. In soccer, video tests (Furley & Memmert, 2015; Memmert, 2010a, b; Memmert, Hüttermann, & Orliczek, 2013) and game test situations (Memmert, 2004a, b, 2006b, 2010b) were developed to capture these three factors.

- **Originality:** The unusual tactical decision actions can be evaluated by soccer experts.

- **Flexibility:** The variety of tactical decision actions is determined by the variety of actions or responses of the soccer players.

- **Fluidity:** The number of tactical decision actions that soccer players generate for a particular situation constellation.

In the last few years, national and international empirically based research programs have led to the development of numerous methodological possibilities for soccer-specific training of tactical creativity (for an overview: Memmert, 2012, 2015). Meanwhile, neuroscience approaches are also increasingly used to better understand the emergence and processes of tactical creativity (Fink et al., 2018, 2019; Rominger et al., 2020, 2021).

On a methodological level, the seven principles—or the seven Ds of creativity training in soccer—are: 1) deliberate play, 2) one-dimensional games, 3) diversification, 4) deliberate coaching, 5) deliberate memory (discussed independently in the next chapter), 6) deliberate practice, and 7) deliberate motivation (figure 9). Their arrangement is deliberate and corresponds to chronological order. While the first four principles seem more suitable for child and youth training, all seven principles can also be used in adult training. The Ds can, for example, be considered for teaching soccer-specific tactical content (e.g., basic tactics: Memmert & Breihofer, 2006; Memmert, Thumfart, & Uhing,

2014), but also basic tactics for all sports (general ball school: Roth & Kröger, 2011; ball school, racket games; Roth, Kröger, & Memmert, 2002; ball school throwing games: Roth, Memmert, & Schubert, 2006).

*Figure 8: The seven Ds of tactical creativity training in soccer (Memmert, 2014).*

## 3.5.1 Deliberate Play

Unguided and unrestricted experimentation in play and unstructured situations during childhood is called deliberate play (Côté, Baker, & Abernethy, 2007). Movement biography studies and field experiments indicate that deliberate play in childhood and adolescence has influenced the creativity of current national team players and Bundesliga players. Unaccompanied action can thus lead to a wide variety of responses.

### 3.5.2 One-Dimensional Games

With one-dimensional games, you can develop a general and soccer-specific tactical creativity which can be characterized as follows (Memmert, 2004a, b, Memmert & Roth, 2003):

- Focusing on one basic tactic (not several!)

- Defining clear role distributions in the game

- Defining specific framework situations

- Guarantee of repeating framework situations

- Guarantee of consistent framework situations

- Guarantee of high repetition rates

- Guarantee of different teammates and opponents through systematic rotations

### 3.5.3 Diversification

Tactical creativity can be trained with varied sports game independent training, in which children and teenagers solve tactical tasks with hands, feet, and hockey sticks. Dealing with many different sports-specific situations allows them to gain a variety of movement experiences (Memmert, 2006b). For the creation of original solutions, it is essential for children and adolescents to play with various balls at a relatively young age in the movement biography, and learn to act in different types of games with different motor requirements in order to think about these kinds of situations repeatedly.

### 3.5.4 Deliberate Coaching

A broad focus of attention is necessary to perceive sudden subjects such as free players, who can be the starting point for original solutions (Memmert, 2005). Fewer instructions from the coaches (deliberate memory) can help children and adolescents to generate creative and varied solutions. Young soccer players, who are constantly confronted with attention-grabbing instructions in the training sessions, can be distracted through the interruption. To promote tactical creativity, it is not advisable for the trainer to continually stop the practice game and give tactical instructions to the players, as these instructions limit the focus of attention (Furley & Memmert, 2007).

### 3.5.5 Deliberate Motivation

Results from social psychology suggest that creative performances can be manipulated by instructions. This can happen, for example, if the type of instruction influences the emotional state of the respondent during the task. Memmert and colleagues (2013) were able to show that tactical creativity in soccer also benefits from a focus on hope (promotion focus; i.e., when the goal of the task is aimed after as an excellent condition). The opposite would be a prevention focus created by the purpose of avoiding a foul. Overall, the results indicate that coaches who use appropriate instructions to promote the focus ("Your goal is to play every third ball into the seam!" instead of "You must play every third ball into the seam!") support the generation of creative solutions in soccer-specific situations.

### 3.5.6 Deliberate Practice

To effectively improve specific individual performance criteria, guided acting in exercise-centred and structured situations is called deliberate practice (Côté, Baker, & Abernethy, 2007). Research demonstrates that competitive athletes need more than 10 years of intensive, sport-specific, and high-quality training in order to have a chance to become top athletes (Ericsson, Krampe, & Tesch-Römer, 1993; for an opposite position, see Hambrick & Meinz, 2011; Macnamara, Hambrick, & Oswald, 2014). Memmert, Baker, and Bertsch (2010) proved that future highly creative soccer players trained much longer in soccer than less creative soccer players. Thus, deliberate practice seems to be a necessary but not sufficient feature to promote tactical creativity, especially in late childhood and early adolescence.

# 3.6 Working Memory

The pivot of conscious information processing is working memory, in which a limited amount of information relevant to the current activity can be processed (overview: Baddeley, 2007). The capacity and general functioning of the working memory are of particular importance for cognition in soccer (for an overview, Furley & Memmert, 2010).

### What Is Working Memory?

For many cognitive tasks, memory is essential in providing objectives, important attention results, information retrieved from the long-term memory, intermediate results of processing, and coordinating the processing of all this information. Almost all cognitive processes require the temporary, demand-oriented availability of information. Working memory is thus a key system for understanding complex cognitive performance (Engle, 2002).

### Definition

**working memory**—A term used by cognitive psychologists to "describe the ability to simultaneously maintain and process targeted information. As the name implies, the concept of working memory reflects at its core, a kind of memory, but it is much more than just a memory, because it is a memory at work and in the service of complex perception." (Conway et al., 2007)

Although the individual capacity of an athlete's working memory does not seem to influence the different performances in sports games (Furley & Memmert, 2015), coaches should avoid sharing too much information in a tactical briefing or discussion due to the limited capacity of working memory (Cowan, 2001, 2005). In addition, it should be noted that the working memory is used to a greater extent when learning new skills (tactical, cognitive, and motor) than in later stages of competence (Maxwell, Masters, & Eves, 2003; Schmidt & Wrisberg, 2004; cf. figure 9).

In contrast to novices, experts do not store specific events (e.g., the paths of individual players, tactical constellations) as individual information units but rather as tactical patterns of player constellations (chunking processes).

On the one hand, this facilitates and improves the early anticipation of significant situation constellations (Williams & Ericsson, 2005). On the other hand, the limited capacity of working memory is not as quickly exhausted by experts as by novices. It can thus be used to perceive different situation constellations or sophisticated tactical decision-making processes (Williams, Hodges, North, & Barton, 2006).

The general functioning of the working memory (i.e., the fact that information in the working memory is processed, manipulated, and structured at short notice [Conway et al., 2007]) has significant consequences for decision-making training in sports games. Recent studies (Furley & Memmert, 2013) have shown that the activated contents of the working memory direct the attention focus of an athlete by drawing attention to the objects in the field of vision to which the contents of the working memory refer. It has also been shown that the working memory capacity allows predictions of which athletes can focus their attention by masking task-irrelevant stimuli, thus avoiding disruption (Furley & Memmert, 2012).

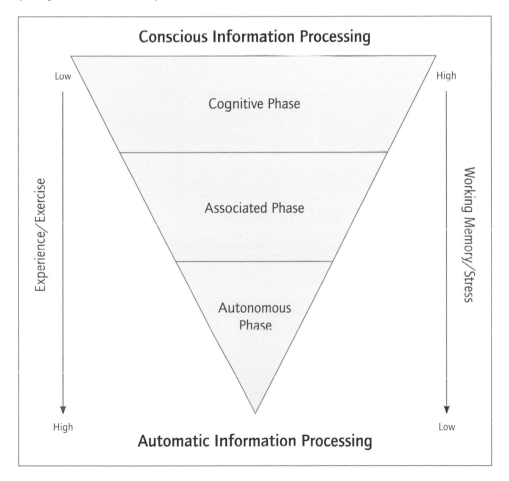

*Figure 9: Working memory demands in tactical learning depend on the level of expertise of the athlete (Furley & Memmert, 2010).*

As a result, particularly for the methodological principle of deliberate memory as one of the seven Ds, in a positive case, the trainer's instructions can direct the athlete's attention focus, thus facilitating tactical/creative decisions. In the negative case, athletes increasingly resort to irrelevant information from the trainer that prevents optimal choices from being made through unfavorable attention control in the specific situation (Furley, Memmert, & Heller, 2010).

# 4 DIAGNOSTICS OF COGNITIONS

In literature nowadays, an almost unmanageable flood of cognitive tests exists. They range from scientifically proven to pure software products that do not meet scientific criteria. In the following, no general overview is given. However, selected methods developed in recent years at the Institute for Training Science and Sports Informatics and used in studies and practice are presented. Four laboratory tests and four field tests are also offered as examples.

## 4.1 Laboratory Tests

In the following, four cognitive test procedures are presented, which have been developed and used in various projects at the Institute for Training Science and Sports Informatics. After the testing, the athletes received a summary of their test results compared to different sport-specific test subject groups' results (see figure 10).

## Cognitive Skills

| | Attention window (static) | Working memory capacity | Susceptibility to distraction | Divided attention (dynamic) |
|---|---|---|---|---|
| | The *attention window task* determines the perceivable visual with one look at the field (in degrees), limited by the individual maximum horizontal (h) and vertical (v) alignment. | The *working memory span test* measures an athlete's ability to focus his attention on the task at hand without being distracted by other thoughts. | The *perceptual load test* measures the extent to which athletes are distracted by external stimuli (plus/minus values = higher/lower distraction), which are completely irrelevant to their task—low (n)/high (h) perceptual load. | The *motion option tracking test* measures up to which speed athletes can track several, relevant, moving objects. |
| NN<br>NN | h     *<br>v | 55 % | n -31<br>h 68 | * |
| Basketball<br>*German national league* | h 38,0<br><br><br>v 36,0 | 91 % | n 68<br><br><br>h 56 | 1.251 |
| Table tennis<br>*German national league* | h<br><br><br>v | 87 % | n -24<br><br><br>h -9 | 1.204 |
| Golf<br>*German national league* | h<br><br><br>v | 62 % | h 48<br>n -35 | |
| Soccer<br>*German national league* | h 40,0<br><br><br>v 33,0 | 87 % | n 54<br><br><br>h 33 | 1.274 |
| Soccer<br>*U15* | h 24,0<br>v 18,0 | 57 % | n 19<br>h -8 | 1.013 |
| Soccer<br>*U12/U13* | h 5,0<br>v 4,7 | 57 % | h 23<br>n -8 | 963 |
| Tennis<br>*U10* | h 4,8<br>v 5,5 | 55 % | n 12<br>h 26 | * |

Training recommendation:

Test date:

*Not recorded

*Figure 10: Presentation of the results of all four elementary cognitions of an exemplary athlete combined with the group mean values of individual other samples (sport discipline, age, expertise).*

## 4.1.1 Attention Window Test

The attention window test (AWT) by Hüttermann, Memmert, Simons, and Bock (2013) can be used to assess the individual's range of attention. During each test phase, players are instructed to fix a central point and try to detect a grey triangle within circle and square distractors. For several attempts, the target will appear at different distances from the attachment point (10, 20, and 30 degrees), along with one of eight equally disputed radial lines from a square in the centre of the display (45-degree distance) (see figure 11). This random display is shown for 12 ms, followed by a coloured mask (100 ms).

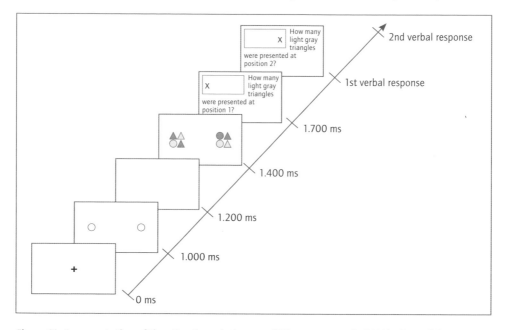

*Figure 11: Representation of the attention window test (Hüttermann et al., 2012). The task is to perceive two stimuli peripherally at the same time. The maximum, still perceptible distance between the stimuli in horizontal, vertical, and diagonal directions is measured, and a maximum attention window is determined.*

After the masking, the players are asked to indicate how many grey triangles they had just seen in the different locations, depending on the orientation of the objects. The participants must complete 180 attempts. This task measures how well people can handle objects far from fixation (Hüttermann, Simons, & Memmert, 2014). The dependent measure is the point distribution of the diagonal attention window and the division of the total value by the number of dimensions (i.e., three).

## 4.1.2 Working Memory Span Test

The established working memory span test of Conway, Kane, Bunting, Hambrick, Wilhelm, and Engle (2005) measures the athlete's ability to draw attention to the task without being distracted by other thoughts. The processing task is to count certain forms between the distractors and then remember the counts for later memory recall. Each task contains randomly arranged dark blue circles, green circles, and dark blue squares (see figure 12). The task is to count the dark blue circles out loud and then announce the total number of circles at the end. After two to six tasks, a reminder mask appears in which the players have to enter their memorised totals precisely in the order in which they were displayed (see Kane, Hambrick, Tuholski, Wilhelm, Payne, & Engle 2004, for a detailed description).

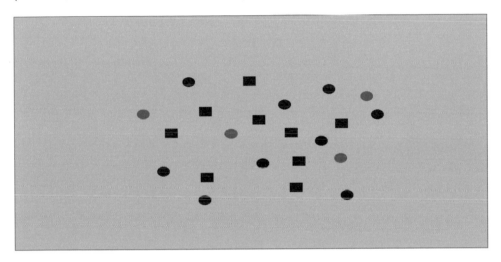

*Figure 12: Representation of a display of the working memory span test by Conway et al. (2005). The player has to count out loud all dark blue circles between the distractors (green circles and dark blue squares) and then memorise the totals for a later memory recall.*

The simplicity of this counting task permits it to be performed with almost any player. The margin score is a subtotal (see Conway et al. 2005) that represents the sum of all successfully recovered items—those items correctly retrieved from a set of two items are worth 2 points, and those correctly retrieved from a collection of six items are worth 6 points—divided by the maximum possible score. The test consists of 15 attempts. The dependent measure is the evaluation of the correctly memorised objects as a per cent.

## 4.1.3 Perceptual Load Test

The perceptual load test by Beck and Lavie (2005) measures cognitive inhibition since it determines the extent to which players are distracted by stimuli that are entirely irrelevant to their task. The players perform the soccer-specific perceptual load task (Furley, Memmert, & Schmid, 2013), which starts with two example blocks (a high and a low cognitive distraction load), followed by eight experimental blocks that alternate between low and high load blocks (figure 13). All players start with one block under a high load. Before each measurement, a fixation cross of 1,000 ms is displayed in the middle of the screen, followed by the task display with the soccer-specific arrangement and the distraction manoeuvre. The task indicators are shown for 100 ms. Players are instructed to ignore the distraction and indicate as quickly and accurately as possible which player has the ball. The distraction manoeuvre is always shown at a fixing point (Beck & Lavie, 2005). The participants react to the target stimuli by pressing a key. A new task is triggered by the player's reaction or omissions within two seconds. After each attempt, feedback on the quality of the answers or omissions is given by means of a computer sound. After each block, the participants are reminded of the critical assignment. The test consists of 160 attempts. The dependent measure is the reaction time of the perceptual stress related to the state of low and high distraction.

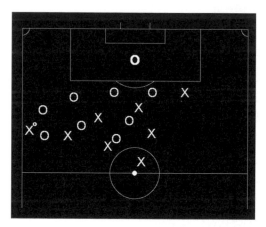

Figure 13: Representation of a display of the soccer-specific perceptual load task by Furley et al. (2013). The players must ignore the distraction (0 in the penalty area) and indicate as fast and as accurately as possible which player is in possession of the ball (0 = defence or X = offence).

## 4.1.4 Multiple Object Tracking Test

The multiple object tracking test for movement tracking measures the velocity at which players are still able to track multiple relevant moving objects (Alvarez & Franconeri, 2005; see figure 14). 3D multiple object tracking training has positive effects on passing decisions (Romeas, Guldner, & Faubert, 2016), but no significant transfer effects on other visual or executive functions (Scharfen & Memmert, 2021).

The players observe the positions of a series of moving circles on a computer monitor. The display initially contains four green and three blue circles. After three seconds in sleep mode, the blue items turn green and are identical to the targets (green circles), and all circles begin to move as players try to track the positions of the initial green items. The test is adaptable so that the speed thresholds and the number of attempts depend on the players' abilities. After eight seconds, the circles stop, and players must mark the three formerly blue circles. Performance is defined by the number of correctly tracked and marked circles. This task shows individual differences in the ability to divide and maintain attention on several independently moving objects (see figure 14c), but no significant transfer effects on other visual or executive functions (Scharfen & Memmert, 2021).

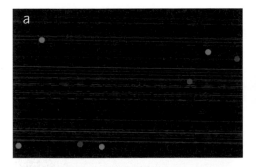

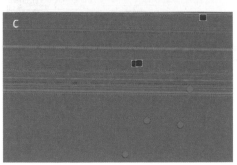

*Figure 14: Representation of the multiple object tracking test (Cavanagh & Alvarez, 2005). The task is to track and recognize several (a) static images for identification, and (b) moving objects at the same time to finally (c) identify them at the end of the test.*

# 4.2 Field Tests

Elementary cognitions are also known as basic tactics in sports games (Memmert, 2004a). As already described in section 3.4, these are basic skills that are of particular importance in many sports games, including tennis, in order to be able to learn the foundation for later sport-specific tactics. Game test situations can make both tactical creativity (Memmert, 2010a, b; Memmert & Roth, 2007) and game intelligence (best solutions) assessable for basic tactical tasks (cf. Memmert, 2010b; Memmert & Roth, 2003; Memmert, 2013). The resulting convergent performance indicators can be used for talent diagnostics in lessons or for grading in physical education classes. During the lesson, it may be helpful to use a video camera to record children's behaviour and then use a video and a scale to assess tactical behaviour. The teacher can also use the developed scale to make the assessment directly at school. For example, four standardised game test situations with their scales for evaluating convergent tactical performance are presented below. They were comprehensively tested on the quality criteria (Memmert, 2004a, b). These diagnostic options use the basic module labels from Memmert (2004a). As these are almost identical in content to the basic modules of Roth and Kröger (2011), they are also listed. Game test situations with the scales for evaluating divergent tactical performances can be read in Memmert (2010a, b) and in Memmert and Roth (2007).

## 4.2.1 Game Test Situation: Moving the Ball to the Goal

In this essential tactic (creating a majority), the players should play the ball in the direction of the goal area. For this purpose, it must be assessed whether the player currently in possession of the ball—if it makes sense—has played the ball in a particular direction of the goal area and if the most considerable possible distance has been bridged (first evaluation criterion). Furthermore, the children's decisions should be evaluated under consideration of the situation (second evaluation criterion).

From these two components, an overall judgment on the performance of the individual can be derived. In this game test situation, only the player active on the ball is evaluated; it is not considered how well the players offer themselves or orient themselves in a space and how the interaction takes place (figure 15).

*Figure 15: Pitch size = 12 × 8 meters, divided into three equally sized fields; distance between video camera and pitch = 3 meters; starting and finish line.*

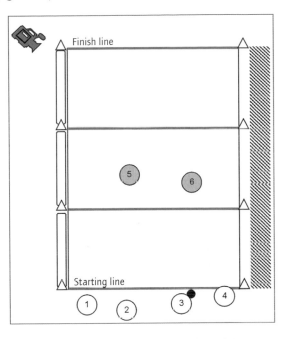

The test situation is performed by teams A and B playing for the possession of the ball. It is important that the attacking team A is 4:2 in the majority. Team A has to transport the ball over the opponent's finish line. The attacking players are allowed to pass the ball but not run with, bounce, or carry it. At each attempt, all players of team A are behind the starting line, whereas the players of the defending team B are in the middle of the field. Each attempt begins with a teacher or trainer signal once both teams are correctly positioned. The player line-ups of the teams are changed twice counterclockwise after each formation has received six attacks. Thus, each player has 12 attacks with different teammates. The evaluation takes place via an approved scaling (see table 5).

*Table 5: Scaling of the basic tactic: Moving the ball to the goal (Memmert, 2004a)*

| Play towards the goal area (quality of solution) | Optimal distance minimization | Scaling | Examples |
|---|---|---|---|
| Optimal | Optimal, > 8 m (2 fields) | 10 | Whenever possible, the player played the ball in the direction of the goal area, bridging as much distance as possible. |
| Optimal | Optimal, > 4 m (1 field) | 9 | The player almost always played the ball in the direction of the goal area, bridging a large distance. |
| Optimal | Optimal, < 4 m (1 field) | 8 | The player usually played the ball in the direction of the goal area, bridging a large distance. |
| Good (better alternative exists) | Average, > 2 m | 7 | The player often played the ball in the direction of the goal area, bridging an average distance. |
| Good (better alternative exists) | Satisfying, < 2 m | 6 | The player often played the ball in the direction of the goal area, bridging a satisfactory distance. |
| Satisfying (better alternative exists) | Average, > 2 m | 5 | The player relatively often played the ball in the direction of the goal area, bridging an average distance. |
| Satisfying (better alternative exists) | Satisfying, < 2 m | 4 | The player relatively rarely played the ball in the direction of the goal area, bridging a satisfactory distance. |
| Insufficient (chose a bad possibility) | Average, < 4 m | 3 | The player rarely played the ball in the direction of the goal area, bridging an average distance. |
| Insufficient (chose a bad possibility) | Average, > 1 to 4 m | 2 | The player almost never played the ball in the direction of the goal area, bridging an average distance. |
| Insufficient (choose a bad possibility) | Satisfying, < 1 m | 1 | The player almost never played the ball in the direction of the goal area, bridging only a satisfactory distance. |

## 4.2.2 Game Test Situation: Interplay

Within the basic tactical game test situation of interplay (cooperative possession of the ball), the ball must be played to a teammate quickly and according to the problem. Two tactical components are evaluated: decision quality and decision time. In decision quality, the spatial decision performance is assessed to determine how well the players can play to free teammates according to the situation. This evaluation considers whether the children are taking advantage of opportunities to play a ball at the right moment while under pressure. The second component—decision time—evaluates whether the players can find adequate solutions in terms of time or at which speed a ball is played. Again, only the player active on the ball is evaluated. The result represents an overall assessment of the individual tactical performance in terms of decision quality and decision time.

Figure 16 illustrates the performance with five players. The four attackers stand in the marked fields and are not allowed to leave them. Furthermore, a defending player controls the rest of the field and is not permitted to enter the four squares. The task of the four attackers is to pass a ball as often and as quickly as possible in one minute. Diagonal passes are not allowed, so the player in possession of the ball has a choice out of two pass options. The defending player's task is to avoid the passing of his opponents. After he succeeds, the ball is rereleased. The attackers cannot play the ball over the defending player using a high pass.

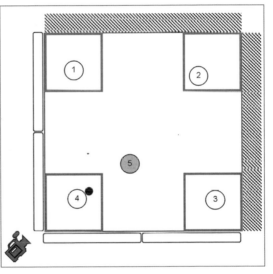

Figure 16: Pitch size = 3.60 x 3.60 meters; side lengths of the four square pitches = 1.0 meters; distance of the video camera (on a mat trolley) to the pitch = 6 meters.

After one minute, the positions are changed according to a given rotation direction. Thus, each player has four minutes to attack (see table 6).

*Table 6: Scaling of the basic tactic: Interplay (Memmert, 2004a)*

| Correctness of decision Adequateness of passing (error/quality) | Decision time/velocity | Scaling | Examples |
|---|---|---|---|
| Always optimal (No errors) | Slightly delayed | 10 | Player played one critical situation optimally and as fast as possible. |
| (Few errors) | Never delayed | | |
| Always optimal (No errors) | Slightly/significantly delayed | 9 | Player played 1-2 critical situations optimally, but often with a slight delay. |
| (Few errors/critical) | Not delayed at all | | |
| Mostly optimal (> 85 %) (Few errors/critical) | Significantly delayed | 8 | Player played the ball with a significant delay and made few errors. |
| (Few errors/critical) | Never/slightly delayed | | |
| Mostly optimal (Few errors/critical) | Significantly delayed | 7 | Player played the ball with a slight delay and made few mainly critical errors. |
| (Few, mainly critical errors) | Never/slightly delayed | | |
| Mainly good (> 70 %) (Few, mainly critical errors) | Significantly delayed | 6 | Player played the ball as fast as possible and made a couple of partly gross errors. |
| (Few critical and gross errors) | Never/slightly delayed | | |
| Mainly good (Few critical and gross errors) | Significantly delayed | 5 | Player played the ball with a slight delay and made a couple of gross errors. |
| (Few, mainly gross errors) | Never/slightly delayed | | |
| Often bad (> 60 %) (Several, mainly critical errors) | Significantly delayed | 4 | Player played the ball with a significant delay and made a couple of gross errors. |
| (Several critical and gross errors) | Never/slightly delayed | | |

| Correctness of decision Adequateness of passing (error/quality) | Decision time/velocity | Scaling | Examples |
|---|---|---|---|
| Often bad (Several critical and gross errors) | Significantly delayed | 3 | Player played the ball with a slight delay and made many critical and gross errors. |
| (Several, mainly gross errors) | Slightly delayed | | |
| Very often bad (<60 %) (Many critical and gross errors) | Significantly delayed | 2 | Player played the ball with significant delay and made many gross errors. The decision-making was barely recognizable. |
| (Several, mainly gross errors) | Never/slightly delayed | | |
| Very often bad (<=50 %) (Many gross errors) | Independent of the decision time | 1 | Player played the ball randomly and made many gross errors. |

## 4.2.3 Game Test Situation: Using Gaps

In this basic tactical game test situation (detecting gaps), the players have to identify gaps and then use them appropriately and according to the game situation. It is therefore assessed whether or not the players have recognised the *optimal gap*. The players must play in their rows if there is no gap in a particular situation. Again, only the player in contact with the ball is evaluated. There is no evaluation of how well the players offer or orient themselves in a space or how they interact with one another.

The attacking team consisting of four players is divided into two players in two attacking zones (figure 17). The defending team consists of three players and acts in the midfield. The defenders are not allowed to leave their zone. Furthermore, the attacking teams are not allowed to enter the defending area. The attacking players have to keep their positions (left or right) and are not allowed to run with the ball. Passing

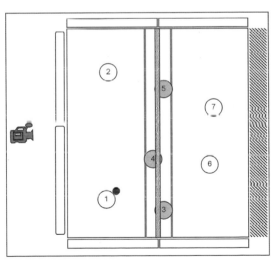

*Figure 17: Pitch size = 8 x 7 meters; width of the middle zone = 1 meter; height of the construction site tape above the middle zone = 1.50 meters; distance of the video camera to the pitch = 8 meters.*

within the two attacking teams is permitted. The defending team always turns towards the player in possession of the ball. After two minutes, the positions are systematically changed so that each player is in an attacking position twice during the game (see table 7).

*Table 7: Scaling of the basic tactic: Using gaps (Memmert, 2004a)*

| Quality of solutions to the situation (using gaps or passing) | Quality of situation | Scaling | Examples |
|---|---|---|---|
| Optimal | Difficult situation | 10 | Even in difficult situations player made optimal use of the gap or passed to a player with a clearer gap. |
| Optimal | Moderate situation | 9 | In moderate situations player made optimal use of the gap except for a few critical decisions. |
| Optimal | Easy situation | 8 | In easy situations player almost always made optimal use of the gap and played against a weak defense. |
| Good, only one better alternative exists | Difficult situation | 7 | In difficult situations player almost always made optimal use of the gap. |
| Good, only one better alternative exists | Moderate situation | 6 | In easy and difficult situations, player made optimal use of the gap except for a few critical decisions. |
| Satisfying, two better alternatives exist | Moderate situation | 5 | In moderate situations player made several critical decisions but no serious errors. |
| Satisfying, two better alternatives exist | Easy situation | 4 | In easy situations player made some serious errors, but usually recognized the gaps correctly. |
| Insufficient, bad possibility was chosen | Difficult situation | 3 | In difficult situations player made several bad decisions, but no serious errors. |
| Insufficient, bad possibility was chosen | Moderate situation | 2 | In moderate and easy situations player made many critical decisions. |
| Insufficient, bad possibility was chosen | Easy situation | 1 | In easy situations player made several serious errors. |

## 4.2.4 Game Test Situation: Creating a Majority

In this standardised game test situation (offering & orienting), players aim to reach an optimal position on the pitch at the right time (see figure 18). Therefore, the criterion to be evaluated is adequate positioning in the game. Consequently, the players who do not play the ball are evaluated. In contrast to the previous game test situations, the evaluation does not include whether the player passed successfully, bridged a distance, or was orientated toward the goal. Furthermore, the difficulty of the situation is evaluated. The result represents an overall judgment of the individual performance in relation to the positioning in space.

An attacking team A and a defending team B—each consisting of three players—play against each other. The task of the attacking team A is to pass the ball as often as possible and not run with the ball. Team B tries to block the passing of the ball. The defending players must keep a distance of two meters from the ball carrier. At the beginning of the game or after an intercepted ball from a defender, an attacker with a ball must be in a predefined starting square. The remaining players can freely move around the pitch. After every two minutes, the players from the three teams are systematically rotated so that each player is attacked twice with different partners during the game test (see table 8).

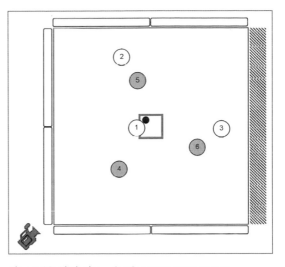

Figure 18: Pitch size = 9 x 9 meters; start square size = 1 x 1 meter; distance of video camera to pitch = 4 meters.

Alternatively, the basic tactic (offer and orient) can be tested here with a stronger reference to the backstroke games using a volleyball net (cf. Roth, Kroger, & Memmert, 2002, p. 70, game form "service game").

*Table 8: Scaling of the basic tactic: Offering and orienting (Memmert, 2004a)*

| Quality of performance (adequate positioning in space) | Quality of situation | Points | Examples |
|---|---|---|---|
| Optimal, always available | Rather difficult | 10 | The player always chose the optimal position in a rather difficult situation and thus always gave the player in possession of the ball the opportunity to pass to him. |
| Optimal, always available | Rather easy | 9 | The player always chose the optimal position in a rather easy situation and thus always gave the player in possession of the ball the opportunity to pass to him. |
| Almost optimal, almost always available | Rather difficult | 8 | The player almost always chose the optimal position in a rather difficult situation and thus mostly gave the player in possession of the ball the opportunity to pass to him. |
| Almost optimal, almost always available | Rather easy | 7 | The player almost always chose the optimal position in a rather easy situation and thus mostly gave the player in possession of the ball the opportunity to pass to him. |
| Good, frequently available | Rather difficult | 6 | The player frequently chose the optimal position in a rather difficult situation and thus mostly gave the player in possession of the ball the opportunity to pass to him. |
| Satisfying, irregularly available | Rather easy | 5 | The player irregularly chose the optimal position in a rather easy situation and thus sometimes gave the player in possession of the ball the opportunity to pass to him. |
| Inadequate, almost never available | Rather difficult | 4 | The player almost never chose the optimal position in a rather difficult situation and thus rarely gave the player in possession of the ball the opportunity to pass to him. |
| Inadequate, almost never available | Rather easy | 3 | The player almost never chose the optimal position in a rather easy situation and thus rarely gave the player in possession of the ball the opportunity to pass to him. |
| Insufficient, never available | Rather difficult | 2 | The player never chose the optimal position in a rather difficult situation and thus never gave the player in possession of the ball the opportunity to pass to him. |
| Insufficient, never available | Rather easy | 1 | The player never chose the optimal position in a rather easy situation and thus never gave the player in possession of the ball the opportunity to pass to him. |

# 5 GAMES FOR COGNITIVE TRAINING

# 5.1 Anticipation Games

## 5.1.1 Reading Serves

### Set-up

Player A serves and player B returns. The server is marked at relevant observation points (information-rich areas) for anticipation. This works best with coloured kinesiotape (mark a right-handed player on the left wrist and left and right shoulders and hips). There should be a good colour contrast with the clothing.

### Execution

The trainee is the returner B. He must try to read A's serves as well as possible by anticipating his movements. It is important that the returner decides on a side before the hitting point of the server, because in this way the anticipation is trained particularly well and the reaction speed takes a back seat. Attention should be focused on the entire movement pattern of the server. The markings should help to perceive and absorb as much information as possible.

## Variations

The server moves further into the court to put the returner under greater time pressure. It is advisable to move forward one racket length at a time until the return player is optimally challenged and can only reach the ball if he anticipates where the serve will go.

# 5.1.2 Reading Smashes

## Set-up
Player A is marked at the relevant observation points (information-rich areas) for anticipation. This works best with a coloured kinesiotape (mark a right-handed player on the left wrist and on the left and right shoulders and hips). There should definitely be a good colour contrast with the clothing.

## Execution
Player A stands on the baseline and player B plays a very high, steep lob as the first ball, which should come up in the back third of the court. Player A should bounce the ball once and then play it as an overhead shot. Player B takes a defensive position well behind the baseline from the start and tries to see where A will hit the lob. Player B must try to read A's balls as well as possible. It is also important here that B decides on a side before A hits the ball. Attention should be focused on A's overall movements. The markings on the information-rich areas also serve as help and orientation here.

## Variations
* The lob is played a little shorter and bounces once before A smashes the ball.

* The ball is hit from the air as a smash.

## 5.1.3 Reading Attacking and Passing Shots

### Set-up

Players A and B position themselves centrally on the baseline. Both players are marked with tape at relevant observation points (information-rich areas; a right-handed player on the left shoulder, a left-handed player on the right shoulder). There should be a colour contrast with the clothing.

### Execution

The ball is played short to the T-line by either coach T or player B. The ball is played from the open hitting position. Player A should attack the short ball alternately with an open and closed stance.

Player B anticipates which corner A will attack and tries to pass player A at the net. Player A, in turn, is to anticipate where B will hit the passing ball to finish the point with a volley. After 5-10 repetitions, the roles are reversed. It is not allowed to play a lob.

### Variation

• Lobs are allowed.

# 5.1.4 Cover the Net

## Set-up
Player A stands about one racket length in front of the T-line at the net. Player B is marked at the information-rich areas with coloured tape and takes a neutral position at the baseline. Coach T is feeding balls from the basket to the corners.

## Execution
Coach T plays two balls from the center alternately into the courts D and A. Player A positions himself at the net slightly to the side and does not interfere with the first ball, but only observes, in particular, how B comes out of the advantage corner. The second ball is played into the run of player B so that he can hit a hard forehand passing shot. Player A has the task of anticipating the correct corner. It is important that A makes his covering behavior at the net as true to the match and dynamic as possible.

## Variations
- Lobs are allowed.

- Angle balls are allowed.

- The coloured markers are removed from player B.

## 5.1.5 Three-Zone Game

### Set-up

The service area is divided into three zones. Server B should be marked at the information-rich areas.

### Execution

Server B gives a hint before the serve, in which field the serve does not come. Return player A tries to read the serve.

### Variations

- Return player A is also given a direction for the return.

- The coloured marks are removed from the server.

## 5.1.6 Slice or Not

Forehand slice!

### Set-up

For this exercise, no other equipment is necessary except for the balls.

### Execution

Players A and B play a rally through the middle. Both players have two tasks: to intersperse forehand and backhand slice into the rally, and to recognize their partner's slice as early as possible and call out "Slice!"

### Variations

- In addition to the slice, A and B should also play drop shots, which should be recognized as early as possible.

- Besides the slice and the stop, A and B should recognize another slice variation as early as possible: the slice attack ball.

## 5.1.7 Estimate Trajectory

### Set-up

Coach T positions himself at the height of the net. Players A and B face each other on the baseline.

### Execution

Players A and B hit the balls through the middle. Player B has to see as early as possible how long the ball is going to be and, before it passes the net, announce aloud his assessment: red, yellow, or green. The coach's role is to monitor whether the ball has already passed the net when A makes his assessment. He can indicate to the players the moment when the ball crosses the net by visual or acoustic signs.

### Variations

*   The exercise is performed in a cross duel.

*   In addition to the length, the zone (A, B, C, or D) in which the ball will bounce is to be called by one of the players (e.g., red and A).

# 5.2 Perception Games

## 5.2.1 Stick With Your Decision

### Set-up
It is played 2:2 on a doubles court. The teams take the usual basic doubles positions.

### Execution
Return player C has the task to play the returns cross court and not to be distracted by the activity of the opponent's net player B. Even if the latter moves inwards, this should be ignored, and the return played cross court.

### Variations
• The net player moves a bit further out to cover the side line.

• The returner plays down the line although the net player has positioned himself there.

## 5.2.2 Stay Focused

### Set-up

Points are played on the single court one against one. The form of the game can be chosen freely.

### Execution

During the ball exchange, a disturbance is deliberately caused (e.g., a ball is rolled into the court by coach T while B returns). The players should block out all irrelevant information as best as they can.

### Variations

- Noise is caused by other players (e.g., cell phone ringing, shouting, or loud music).

- It happens frequently that players perceive calls from a spectator in a match and are distracted by them. A simple way of training for this would be to play a training match with a chair referee and occasionally have a spectator deliberately call "Out!" while the players are not distracted in their concentration.

- Camera flashes can also be used as a distraction.

- One of the players is instructed to be particularly motivated/excited or particularly disinterested/unmotivated. The training player must not be influenced by the body language of the other. It is irrelevant information for his own game.

- Player A is instructed during a training match to mime being injured or to feign cramps. Player B is not informed of this. Coach T and player A observe together how B handles the situation.

## 5.2.3 Observation I

### Set-up

This exercise is about observing the opponent (e.g., their foot position). It is advisable to mark certain areas that are to be particularly noticed with coloured tape or different socks (left foot blue, right foot red).

### Execution

Players A and B hit balls through the middle or play points. Player A is given the task of carefully observing whether player B hits his forehand with an open or closed foot position and informs coach T aloud after each stroke. In order to direct the player's perception to the desired observation points, the coloured markings are helpful. Once again, it should be remembered at this point that the sole purpose is to train and direct the perception in order to absorb more information. The interpretation of this information (e.g., from a tactical point of view) would be the next step. The technical implementation is another.

### Variations

- Observe the shoulder rotation of the opponent and whether the upper body is half or fully turned in (possibly make markings).

- Observe the opponent's racket and whether the face is open or closed.

- Observe the position of the shoulders in relation to the hip and feet.

- If the markings are removed, it is much more difficult to direct the perception to the observation points.

## 5.2.4 Observation II

Closed forehand position, so slice!

### Set-up

This game involves the precise perception of certain body regions in the playing partner (e.g., foot position). The difference to the previous exercise is that the trainee no longer says out loud what he sees, but has to implement concrete game tasks through what he observes.

### Execution

Balls are hit through the middle and player A covers three-quarters of the court with his forehand. Whenever player A plays a shot from the closed position, B should recognize this and answer with a slice ball (forehand and backhand).

### Variations

- Player A plays from the baseline and player B plays volleys at the net. If B notices A's closed leg position, he should play a volley stop. Possibly have the point played out.

- Players A and B play long balls from the baseline through the middle. A's task is to open his hitting area from time to time and play a slice (forehand and backhand). B's task is to recognize the open racket face, go into the court, and play A's slice as a volley.

## 5.2.5 Open Court

### Set-up

A and B are playing against C and D on a doubles court. Coach T is on the side of C and D, who both position themselves close to the net for volleying. Player A returns three times on the deuce side and then three times on the advantage side. B positions himself as the front player just in front of the service line and may vary his position slightly between each repetition (more to the right/left/center or in the service area).

### Execution

When the basic positions are taken, coach T serves player A from the T-line. Player A returns the first three serves from the deuce side and the next three from the advantage side. A is free to decide where he returns but is not allowed to play any lobs as returns for the time being. Players C and D, who have already positioned themselves at the net, must try to play volleys into the free spaces. After finishing the first series of returns on the deuce side, player A must sprint to the double outside line on the advantage side and touch it with the left foot (open stroke position and the racket face pointing to the net). Only then does player A start the backstrokes on the advantage side. Then the roles are changed and player B is served.

### Variations

- Lobs are allowed during the return.

- The rallies are played commonly, and each team can score points.

## 5.2.6 Keep It in the Air

### Set-up

Four signal lights (colours can be chosen freely), a tennis racket, and some balloons are needed. The signal lights are placed in a semicircle on the floor in front of the player. The distance between the lights should be chosen according to the level of the player.

### Execution

The player holds up the balloon with the racket and turns off the signal lights with the other hand.

*If no signal lights are available, this exercise can also be simply recreated with coloured cones. The trainer gives a visual signal by pointing to a colour. The player must then touch the cone of the corresponding colour and hold up the balloon with the racket.*

### Variations

- The distances of the signal lights (cones) vary.

- Raise the signal lights (cones) by attaching them to poles.

- Hold the racket in the other hand.

- Use a tennis or method ball (red, orange, green) instead of the balloon to make the exercise more difficult.

## 5.2.7 Striking Through the Center I

### Set-up

Coach T is positioned behind player A, while B takes the position on the opposite baseline.

### Execution

The players hit balls through the middle. The coach moves to stand behind A, either to the left or right corner. B must recognise this and announce where the coach is going.

### Variations

- Instead of playing through the middle, a cross duel is played.

- The coach indicates the direction of the stroke with the racket head (left or right).

- In addition to the direction, the coach also indicates the trajectory (high, medium, or flat) with the racket head, which trainee B should play.

## 5.2.8 Striking Through the Center II

### Set-up

Coach T positions himself on the deuce side slightly to the side in front of player A outside the double line, and B takes the position on the other side of the court on the baseline.

### Execution

Players A and B hit balls through the middle. Coach passes a ball to A with his foot, which he passes back after each shot.

### Variations

- The coach moves to the advantage corner.

- The exercise is played in a cross rally.

- The return pass must be played alternately with the left and right foot.

- The return pass is played with different techniques (inside or outside foot).

- The player is also given a number or colour that is assigned to a particular foot or technique.

## 5.2.9 Move as One

### Set-up

A stretchable rope and four players (A, B, C, and D) are needed for this double exercise. Coach T is positioned on the side of pair A and B.

### Execution

Double points are played. One pair (C and D) starts at the net, while the other (A and B) stands on the baseline. The pair at the net is connected by a stretchable rope and must function as a unit. The coach passes the ball to C and D standing at the net, and the point is played out freely. The only restriction is that the first volley may not be played as a volley stop.

### Variations

- The same exercise is performed without the rope, and the net pairing continues to act as a unit as if connected by an imaginary cord.

- A rope also connects the players on baselines A and B.

- The coach's feed is no longer to the net pair but to the team on the baseline.

## 5.2.10 Turn the Light Off

### Set-up

Two signal lights are needed, each placed on the T-line. The colours to be set are freely selectable.

### Execution

The players hit balls through the middle. When the signal lamp lights up in your half of the court, the player must play a lob, sprint to the signal lamp, turn it off, and return to the baseline as quickly as possible.

### Variations

- The signal light is placed at the net to extend the running distance. The next shot is then taken at the net.

- The signal light is placed about 1 m in front of the baseline. As soon as it lights up, play should continue normally, and the player must do a fitness exercise, such as a push-up, as quickly as possible and turn off the light.

# 5.3 Attention Games

## 5.3.1 Be Aware

**Set-up**

Players A and B position themselves in the single court. Player A is the server. Coach T is on the side of the returning player B. Enough balls are needed to pass.

**Execution**

Player A serves, and the coach or the return player B gives signals with his hand or body, which A has to recognise and interpret quickly. Playing tasks are linked to individual signals.

For example, if B turns his upper body to the right to the deuce side, A must recognise this and hit the ball into the advantage corner.

Further examples:

- Fist of B or T = cross-court for A.

- Open hand of B or T = down the line for A.

- Raise right hand sideways from B or T = slice with backhand and forehand for A.

The server's attention should be quickly drawn to what is happening in the return player's half of the game.

## Variations

- The signal comes only from the coach by giving audible or visual numerical codes (e.g., holding up a sign).

- The coach gives the signal as late as possible, which makes the exercise very difficult and will most likely force A to make many hitting mistakes. Be sure to point out to the player that the training objective is met when he successfully focuses his attention on the task. The quality of the stroke is not the focus, nor is it the content of the training.

- The trainer is positioned in different places on the court (behind the returning player, in the position of a doubles partner, etc.).

## 5.3.2 Step, Step, Split-Step

### Set-up

The game is played either singles or doubles with serve. The server has the task of opening the rally with different variations (e.g., hard serves into the middle, serve and volley, kick serves on the backhand). The returning player must vary his return position, sometimes in the field, sometimes on the line, sometimes far back. The points are played out.

### Execution

The training content is described based on the serve-and-volley game: The goal is to get into an optimal court position and time the split-step as well as possible. To do this, the server must direct his attention to several factors simultaneously (e.g., the opponent's return position, type of stroke [such as block, chip, or full swing], and service speed).

Depending on what the interpretation of these factors reveals, the server should perform his split-step earlier, before the T-line, or closer to the net.

The returner has the task of varying the speed of the return and his position, sometimes in the field, sometimes closer to the line, far back, sometimes chip or slice, to challenge the server again and again to find the optimal timing for his split-step. The points are played to the end.

## Variations

- Serve and the first ball. The server stays on the baseline and tries to find the optimal court position after the service by focusing his attention on as many factors as possible simultaneously (selective attention) and deciding how he will hit the first ball.

- The returning player varies his position only after the server has tossed the ball.

## 5.3.3 Shot Selection

### Set-up

Coach T positions himself with his basket just behind the T-line. Player A stands at the baseline.

### Execution

The coach feeds the balls from the basket with as much variation as possible (e.g., hard, flat, short, long, high, lots of topspin, slice). The player chooses the technique that makes the most sense for him to return the balls. On the one hand, he should direct his attention to the ball and the game situation. Still, on the other hand, the player should also consider his technical repertoire and body position to achieve the individual ideal solution (selective attention).

Communication between coach and player is essential in this form of training, as there can often be several ideal solutions.

## Variations

- The game situations are artificially created by feeding the balls in different ways. The point is played to the end. The more creative the coach and players are, the more exciting the situations can be.

- Feeding the first ball as a drop-shot or lob.

- One player positions himself at the T-line and starts the point from there.

- One player takes up a position with his back to the court, turns around when called, and the point is played out.

## 5.3.4 Get Together

### Set-up

The exercise is played as doubles. Coach T feeds the balls.

### Execution

Each pairing takes their position, with one player on each team outside the doubles area before the coach feeds the ball. The artificially separated pairs should get back into a good doubles formation and court position as quickly as possible.

### Variations

All four players position themselves at the net, with one player per pair again standing outside the doubles court. The coach plays the ball softly and low.

## 5.3.5 Swipe Master

### Set-up

Twelve signal lights (red and yellow) and two tennis balls (one red small court ball and one yellow ball) are needed. The signal lights are attached to a wall or fence. The player holds both balls in his hand.

### Execution

The signal lights light up in random order and colour. The player has the task of putting out the signal by throwing the balls against the lights of the same colour as quickly as possible.

### Variations

* Other ball colours are assigned to the signal light colours (e.g., red light = yellow ball, yellow light = red ball).

* The height at which the signal lights are fixed can be varied.

* The coach plays balls from time to time in addition to the signal lights on A. In this case, the tennis ball always has priority and should be played back by A.

## 5.3.6 Matching Colours

### Set-up

Twelve signal lights (green, red, and blue) and three tennis balls (green, red, and blue) are needed. The signal lights are attached to a wall, fence, or poles. The player stands in front of the lights at a distance of about 2 meters.

### Execution

The signal lights light up in random order and colour. The player should turn off the signal light with the ball in the same colour.

### Variations

*   Other ball colours are assigned to the signal light colours (e.g., red light = blue ball, blue light = green ball, green light = red ball).

*   The distance to the player's wall can be increased.

*   The height of the signal light attachment can be varied.

*   In addition to the signal lights, the coach occasionally plays balls at A. In this case, the tennis ball always has priority and should be played back from A.

## 5.3.7 The Colourful T

### Set-up

Four signal lights (green, red, blue, and yellow), tennis balls, a tennis racket, and two coloured cones (blue and red) are needed. The signal lights are placed in a square close to each other on the floor. Player A stands directly in front of them. The two cones are located to the right and left of the signal lights, and coach T is standing on the other side of the court at the T-line.

### Execution

The signal lights randomly light up in green, red, blue, and yellow. If the signal light is green, the player must put it out by stepping on it. If the signal light is red, then he must run to the red cone. If the signal light is blue, then the player must run to the blue cone. If the signal light is yellow, the player sprints forward, gets a ball from the coach into the T-field, and must play it back sensitively, possibly as a stop.

## Variations

- The colours can be reassigned (e.g., red light means blue cone, blue light means red cone).

- The game square can be enlarged or reduced.

- The side cones are to be approached with side steps.

- The coach also places the cones where the ball should be played back down the line before the player sprints back to the starting position as quickly as possible.

## 5.3.8 One Out of Four

### Set-up

Four signal lights are needed (three are set to the same colour, and the fourth is set as a random colour). The lights (alternatively cones) are arranged in a square. The spacing should be adjusted to the level of the player. Poles as elevation are helpful for variation of the exercise. Player A is positioned between the signal lights.

### Execution

If three signal lights come on in the same colour and the fourth is in a different colour, the player wipes out the one that does not match. If all four light up in the same colour, A does nothing.

### Variations

- Shorten or lengthen the interval in which the lights shine.

- Increase the number of signal lights.

- Have the player perform an additional movement task, such as holding a tennis ball or bouncing a basketball.

## 5.3.9 See the Light

Lob followed by a push-up

### Set-up

Seven signal lights (all of the same colour) and tennis balls are needed. Four signal lights are attached to four poles. Two are placed to the player's left, and two to the player's right on the doubles line. Three more signal lights are placed on the ground in front of the net (front outer corners of the service courts and centre). The player stands on the baseline with a racket and ball.

### Execution

Player A and coach T hit balls through the middle at a medium pace. When a signal lamp lights up that has been placed at the front of the net, A hits the ball back to the coach normally. However, if a signal lamp lights up on his left or right, A must play a lob back to his playing partner and do a fitness exercise, such as a push-up. There is usually enough time for this without any problems.

## Variations

- Variation of fitness exercise (e.g., squat, squat jump).

- If one of the front signal lights up, A must play the ball in a specific direction. For example, if the front left light is on, the ball must be played cross-court; if the middle front signal light is on, the shot should be played down the line.

## 5.3.10 T-Line Tiger

### Set-up

Four to six signal lights (red and blue), enough balls, and two little cones (one in blue and one in red) are needed. The signal lights are placed in a row at the height of the T-line, with the red cone on the baseline on the advantage side and the blue cone on the baseline on the deuce side. Coach T positions himself on the other half of the court.

### Execution

The signal lamps go on in random order in either red or blue. The player wipes out the lights one at a time by running his racket over them. He should move primarily with side steps. After the player has wiped out the last light, he must circle the cone with the colour with which the last signal light was shining. Then coach A plays a ball into the run, which the player should play back variably according to the situation (e.g., winner, slice).

### Variations

- When the last light is on, the player wipes it out and runs to the cone with the colour that the last signal light did not show.

- The colours can also be reassigned, for example, when the last light is green, the player runs to the blue cone.

- Four colours are set for the signal lights: Red light means down the line at the red cone, blue light means down the line at the blue cone, yellow light means cross-court at the red cone, and green light means cross-court at the blue cone.

**Example:**

Red light means go around the red cone and play the ball down the line. If the blue light is on, the player goes around the blue cone and the shot is made down the line.

If the yellow light is on, it means the player should go around the red cone and hit the ball cross-court.

The green light means run around the red cone and hit the ball cross-court.

## 5.3.11 The Traffic Light

### Set-up

Six signal lights (the colours set can be freely chosen), enough balls, rackets, and two poles are needed. Three signal lights are attached to each pole (top, middle, bottom) and placed about 4 m behind the baseline. The distance between the poles should be about 1 m. The player is approximately one racket length behind the poles with the signal lights.

### Execution

Player A wipes out the signal light that comes on and sprints towards the baseline while receiving a ball from the coach slightly off to the side and hitting it back into the opponent's field.

### Variations

*   The position of the signal lights determines the type of stroke (e.g., top left means backhand slice, bottom right means short forehand cross-court). There are six variations; therefore, up to six stroke techniques can be specified.

- The position of the signal lights determines the target where the ball should be hit (e.g., short behind the net, on the T-line, deep to the baseline).

- The position of the signal lights determines both the type of stroke and the target where the ball is to be hit (e.g., with backhand slice short behind the net, with forehand topspin on the T-line, a forehand topspin lob long to the baseline).

## 5.3.12 Z-Ball

### Set-up
A Z-ball is required. This is often called a reaction ball. Players A and B face each other in the half court.

### Execution
Player A throws the Z-ball to B. B must anticipate the bounce of the reaction ball, catch it, and throw it back from where he caught it.

### Variations
*   Partners decide whether the ball is thrown long and fast or short.

*   After the Z-ball bounces, it must be clapped once before the ball is caught.

*   The ball may only be caught with one hand.

*   The ball may only be caught with either the right or left hand.

## 5.3.13 Number Board

### Set-up

Players A and B both take their positions on the baseline. Coach T needs boards or sheets of paper with numbers on them.

### Execution

Player A plays with player B through the middle. After each shot, player A must look to the coach, who holds up a board with a number. The player must then say the number out loud.

### Variations

- Several people hold up several boards at the same time, and the player should notice all of them.

- Points are played, and during the rally, the coach is allowed to suddenly hold up a board with a number.

- The number boards are linked to concrete game tasks; for example, the number seven means that the player must finish the point with the following two shots, play a stop, etc.

## 5.3.14 Double In

### Set-up

Players A and B position themselves diagonally in the deuce court, while C and D face each other diagonally at the net.

### Execution

A and B play cross points against each other at the baseline, while C and D face each other at the net and play volley points. As soon as one of the rallies is over, the point that is not yet finished is played all over the court and finished by all players together.

### Variation

The parallel rallies are played down the line instead of cross-court. As soon as one of the two rallies is finished, the point that is not yet finished is played over the whole court and by all players to the end.

# 5.4 Game Intelligence Games

## 5.4.1 Cross-Court and Down the Line

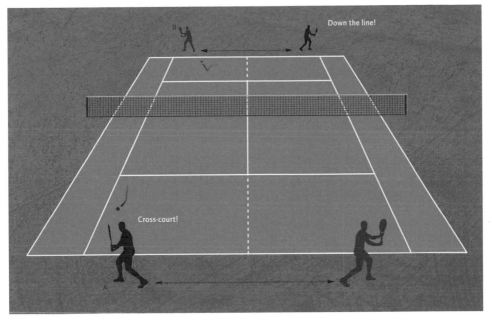

### Set-up
Two players (A and B) are sufficient for this exercise. If the exercise is played in threes or fours, you simply switch after every two points. The court is divided in the middle. In addition, a sufficient number of balls are needed.

### Execution
The game is played to 10 points, during which player A may only play cross-court, and player B may only play down the line. If one of the players succeeds in scoring a winner, he gets three points. Should a player make a drop-shot or come to the net, the rules of playing only cross-court or down the line remain in effect in the basic exercise.

The mutual knowledge of the rough direction where the next ball will be played makes it very difficult to score direct pointsand, therefore, requires particularly creative and intelligent moves or excellent stroke execution. Stroke security is also improved in the process, of course.

## Variations

- The rally is opened with serve and return, with the returner playing cross-court and the server playing down the line. It is advisable to possibly only allow second serves so that it is easier to get into the rally.

- After a drop-shot or a net attack by a player, the instructions to play only cross-court or down the line are cancelled, and the point is played over the entire court to the end.

# 5.4.2 Forehand Duel

## Set-up

Two or four playing partners are optimal for this exercise. The court is divided in the middle. In addition, enough balls are needed.

## Execution

Players A and B stand diagonally opposite each other and play points to 10. Both players may only use their forehand. Otherwise, they lose points. After four points have been played on the deuce side, the players switch to the advantage side. Again, only forehands may be played inside-out. If one of the players is left-handed, one plays the forehand cross-court while the other plays inside-out.

If the exercise is played with four players, players C and D can play their forehand duel on the advantage side, while A and B duel on the deuce side.

## Variations

* Drop-shots and net attacks are allowed, but all balls must be played with the forehand.

* Drop-shots and net attacks are allowed, and the point is played freely across the court. If four players play the exercise, the point is played freely on the respective half of the court.

### 5.4.3 Three-Quarter Forehand

### Set-up

Two playing partners A and B, are optimal for this exercise. One half of the court is divided into three sections. In addition, enough balls are needed.

### Execution

Points are played out to 10. Player A must cover his third with his forehand, but the entire opponent's field is available to him. Player B, on the other hand, is allowed to use his forehand and his backhand, but he must play into the reduced area on A's side.

### Variations

- A is allowed to play at least one backhand per rally.

- B must play exclusively slice on the backhand.

- Drop-shots and net attacks are allowed, and then the point is finished freely.

# 5.4.4 Serve and Volley

## Set-up

This exercise can be done with two, three, or four players. In addition, enough balls are needed.

## Execution

As the server, player A must play serve and volley. The returning player B should capitalise on this knowledge and use it intelligently. In the basic version of this exercise, the coach should tell the server to serve with a maximum of 85-90% speed. The return should be played low to the feet of the server. The goal is to play a volley and a passing shot frequently to get a feel for the game situation. Each player serves four times in a row. The game is played to 20 points.

## Variations

*   The server states, for example, that he will always come forward with a kick serve on the backhand.

*   The returning player will only play softly on A's feet, while A is entirely free in his decisions.

*   It is played with the default of coming forward with the first and second serve. The rest is free.

## 5.4.5 Zones and Heights

### Set-up

The space at the baseline is divided into three overlapping zones (A, B, and C). An elevation should be placed at the net so that there are three different heights (one, two, and three). The exercise can be done with two players, and requires a sufficient number of balls.

### Execution

The players hit balls through the middle at medium height and speed (zone B/height 2). The target is to move into zone A as often as possible and hit the ball flat and fast over the net (zone A/height 1). At the coach's call, the players change their position, for example, to zone C, and hit from there with a higher trajectory (zone C/height 3) until the coach gives another signal.

### Variations

*   Player A stands in zone B (neutral zone) and hits balls of medium hardness and height through the middle. Meanwhile, Player Y plays four shots each in zone A and height 1 and then drops to zone C and plays height 3. After 3-5 minutes, there is a changeover.

- Points are played to 10. For one set, each rally is started in zone A and height 1, the next in zone B and height 2, and in the third set, rallies are started in zone C and height 3.

- The game is played with serve, and the returners determine which trajectory the rally is played in based on their return position.

## 5.4.6 Safety First

### Set-up

Two playing partners A and B, are optimal for this exercise. On one half of the court, a target area with marking lines is laid out in the middle, which should be approximately 1 m from the baseline, as a buffer zone. In the opposite half of the court, two target areas are laid out from the sideline to the centre (each approximately 3 m wide). Coach T stands on the sideline on B's side.

### Execution

Player A hits the balls freely on B's half of the court and aims at the target fields 1 and 2. B's task is to aim for target area 3, which is in the centre of the court. This minimises his risk of errors and does not give A angles that he could use well. For player A, the focus is more on precision, while for B, the focus is on safety and consistency. If a mistake is made, coach T immediately feeds in a new ball to keep the exercise going.

### Variations

- Player B plays deep with a lot of shape to neutralise A.

- Player B uses a lot of slice and flat-bouncing balls to make it difficult for A to build up pressure.

- If A plays into the same court three times in a row, the point is played out freely.

- The point is played out freely if A plays two slice balls in a row.

- Points are played, and the ball must land in one of the target areas. Otherwise, it is counted as a fault. It is recommended to enlarge the target fields considerably to have enough rallies. The precision pressure increases enormously with this variation.

## 5.4.7 C+ Battle

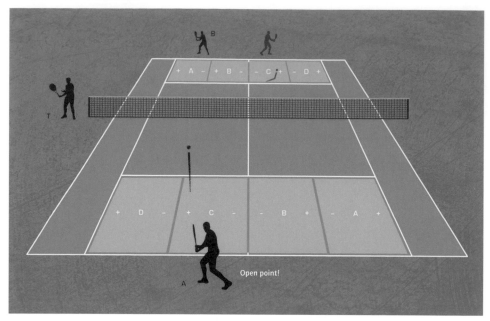

### Set-up

This exercise is ideal for two playing partners. Each player's side of the court is divided into four zones (A, B, C, and D). In addition, the fields can be further refined by using the "+" and "-" signs. The C+ zone should be well marked in both halves of the court.

### Execution

Both players try to hit the C+ target with the backhand and get into a favourable position on the court. A is allowed to stop the rally by no longer playing on C+ but rather on A or B. Then the point is played out freely.

### Variations

- Player A runs around his backhand and plays inside-out on C+. A is free to play an inside-out angle on D+ or a forehand inside-in on A+. The point is then played out freely.

- Both players run around their backhands and play inside-out on C+. A is free to play an inside-out angle or an inside-in forehand. Then the point is played out freely.

- The point is started with the serve, and the return should be aimed at C+. After that, the point is played out freely.

# 5.5 Methodical Notes on Game Creativity

Methodical notes on tactical game creativity training can be found here. These can be used in different game forms or basic tactics.

*Deliberate play:* An unguided game can lead to a greater variety of solutions.

*One-dimensional games:* Games can train individual basic tactics across sports games through a high number of similar situation constellations.

*Diversification:* The use of different motor skills in games can support the training of original solution variations.

*Deliberate coaching:* Instructions that reduce the attention focus of the players should not be used in the games.

*Deliberate motivation:* For the games, hope-based instructions are to be used which increase the generation of unusual solutions.

*Deliberate practice:* In later stages of the learning process, the game can be adapted to the specific needs of football, so that a targeted overlearning of football-specific solution variations can take place.

# 5.6 Working Memory Games

## 5.6.1 Where to Put the Serve?

### Set-up

The service boxes are divided into eight fields of equal size and marked with the numbers one through eight. It is recommended to note the given ball sequences. The following abbreviations have proven themselves in practice: S = slice serve, F = flat serve, K = kick serve.

### Execution

Coach T gives the server a sequence of serves and notes them down. In the following example, this would be four serves. The abbreviated form is provided in parentheses.

First serve: Slice to field five        (S5)

Second serve: Flat to field six        (F6)

Third serve: Kick to field eight        (K8)

Fourth serve: Slice to court one        (S1)

To start, it is recommended to have at least four service variations. The player memorises the coach's instructions as accurately as possible and begins to play the ball sequence. Before each serve, the player must tell the coach how and where he serves. The coach notes whether the player was able to remember the instructions. The number of instructions is to be increased until the server reaches the limits of his ability to remember.

## Variations

- Serve+1: In addition to the serve, the coach specifies how and possibly where the first ball should be played (e.g., if the first ball is to be played cross court into field C+ after the serve, the return comes on the backhand).

- For the returner to practice his working memory, he can be asked after the game sequence whether he could remember where his training partner placed the serves. To complicate this variation, introduce a time limit for recalling serve placement.

## 5.6.2 Cross-Court or Down the Line? Memorise It.

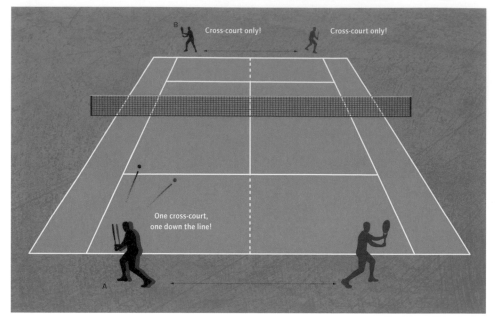

### Set-up

The tennis court is divided lengthwise into two halves.

### Execution

Player A plays one ball cross-court and one ball down the line. Player B plays only cross-court but must count in the same way as player A to change sides in time (rhythm: one cross-court/one down the line). After one minute, player A plays two balls cross-court and one ball down the line (rhythm: two cross-court/one down the line). After another minute, player A plays three balls diagonally and one ball down the line (rhythm: three cross court/one down the line). After another minute, player A plays four balls cross-court and one ball down the line (rhythm: four cross-court/one down the line). Even with increasing fatigue, players should remember where to hit and run.

### Variations

*   Role Reversal: During the exercise, the players' roles are reversed at the coach's call. The player who just played cross-court and down the line now plays cross-court and vice versa.

*   The Stairs: Here, the rhythm is increased very quickly by one cross-court stroke at a time. Player A plays one cross court and one down the line, then two cross-court, one

down the line, then three cross court and one down the line, etc. After three minutes, the roles of the players are to be changed. Alternatively, the parts can be changed after each mistake.

- Mix It Up: In this variation, player A is instructed how to play the stroke down the line. The basic rhythm is two balls cross court and one down the line; then player A has to play the first down the line with flight curve, the second deep with slice, the third flat and hard, and the fourth down the line short on the T-line. After that, the first sequence of variations can be started again, or new ones are given. The exercise is highly complex and demanding.

## 5.6.3 Once Upon a Time

| Set 1 | | | | Set 2 | | | | Set 3 | | |
|---|---|---|---|---|---|---|---|---|---|---|
| Ball | End | Impulse | | Ball | End | Impulse | | Ball | End | Impulse |
| 1 | | | | 1 | | | | 1 | | |
| 2 | | | | 2 | | | | 2 | | |
| 3 | | | | 3 | | | | 3 | | |
| 4 | | | | 4 | | | | 4 | | |
| 5 | | | | 5 | | | | 5 | | |
| 6 | | | | 6 | | | | 6 | | |
| 7 | | | | 7 | | | | 7 | | |
| 8 | | | | 8 | | | | 8 | | |
| 9 | | | | 9 | | | | 9 | | |
| 10 | | | | 10 | | | | 10 | | |
| 11 | | | | 11 | | | | 11 | | |
| 12 | | | | 12 | | | | 12 | | |
| 13 | | | | 13 | | | | 13 | | |
| 14 | | | | 14 | | | | 14 | | |
| 15 | | | | 15 | | | | 15 | | |
| 16 | | | | 16 | | | | 16 | | |
| 17 | | | | 17 | | | | 17 | | |
| 18 | | | | 18 | | | | 18 | | |
| 19 | | | | 19 | | | | 19 | | |

### Set-up

For this exercise, it is recommended that coach T take notes and make a small chart.

### Execution

Points are played from the baseline to 10. If the score is 9, the following point is decisive. A maximum of 19 points can be played.

How the point is started is freely up to the coach and the players. The coach notes down the last stroke of the point during the game. At the end of each round, players must write from memory all the strokes with which the points ended; to increase pressure, set a time limit of 90 seconds. Whoever could remember more should get, for example, five extra points. Ideally, the memory game's incentive should be designed so that the loser of the tennis match can still win in the end.

## Variations

- Best of Three: Match tie-breaks are played to 10. At a score of 9-9, the following point decides. The players have to give the shots that ended the points only after the entire match. Whoever gives more correct answers within two or three minutes is rewarded with a bonus.

- Impulse: In this variation for very advanced players, the focus is no longer on the last stroke but on the one with which a GAME IMPULSE was set (e.g., a drop-shot). The task is to identify the stroke or strokes in a rally that were decisive for the outcome of the rally. Whether the point was won or lost in the process is irrelevant. Ideally, the playing impulses are judged in the same way by the coach and the players ("I played a good angle and only had to finish the point properly afterwards" could be a statement from a player who felt his good angle was the decisive impulse for the rally). It is advisable to work out and identify the impulse shots together with the players.

## 5.6.4 Connect Four

### Set-up

Four targets and enough balls are needed.

### Execution

Coach T assigns fixed numbers to the four targets on the court and gives the player a sequence of how to play on the targets with the numbers (e.g., one, three, two, and four). The player memorises this sequence of numbers and then plays on the marks according to the instructions.

### Variations

- The player must play the immediately finished series again immediately in reverse order.

- The number of given targets is significantly increased (double, triple, quadruple).

- The four targets are assigned colours and symbols in addition to numbers (e.g., four, red, star, one).

# 5.6.5 Let the Ball Bounce

## Set-up
No equipment is needed for this exercise.

## Execution
Coach T plays six balls, and the player is told how many times to bounce the ball (e.g., ball one bounces once, ball two bounces three times, ball three bounces twice, ball four bounces once, ball five bounces twice, and ball six bounces once).

## Variations
*   The numbers are reversed (e.g., one is three and three is one).

*   Colours are used for coding (e.g., green is one, blue is two, and red is three).

*   The specifications are given visually (e.g., by pointing a certain number of fingers).

## 5.6.6 Use Codes

### Set-up

Plenty of balls are needed for this exercise.

### Execution

Coach T stands near the T-line and plays the balls in freely over the entire court, telling the player with a code where to hit the balls (e.g., one for down the line, two for cross-court, and three for a drop-shot). The ball sequence should consist of at least six numbers. The player must remember these and place the balls accordingly.

### Variations

• Besides the numbers, colours, and symbols can also be used as codes, optionally in combination.

• In addition to the cross-court and down the line directions, slice and topspin are also coded.

# 5.6.7 Vary Trajectories

## Set-up

For this exercise, it is recommended to use a net elevation with different colours (green, blue, and red). In one of the variations of this exercise, the court of player X is divided into zones A, B, and C.

## Execution

Coach T stands near the T-line and feeds the balls freely over the entire court, telling the player with a code which trajectory he has to use. For example, green is used for a flat flight curve about one racket length over the net, blue means a medium flight curve (about two racket lengths over the net), and red means a high flight curve (about three racket lengths over the net). The ball sequence should consist of at least six colour codes. The player must remember these and place the balls accordingly.

## Variations

- In addition to the trajectory, the coach also codes the player's court position. In the illustration, A, B, and C are used for this (e.g., A green, B blue, C red, C blue, A red, and B green).

- In addition to colours, numbers and symbols can also be used as codes, optionally in combination.

- In addition to the trajectory, slice and topspin are also coded.

# 5.6.8 Forehand Precision

## Set-up

The court is divided into fields A, B, C, and D. Each field is again divided into plus and minus, where plus always means outward towards the sideline and minus always means inward toward the centre. Player S is at the baseline. Coach T is standing near the T-line. Sufficient balls are needed.

## Execution

The coach gives the player four stroke variations (e.g., ball one: FH cross-court on A+, ball two: FH cross-court on B-, ball three: FH down the line on D+, ball four: FH down the line on C+. The player memorises the coach's instructions and plays the targets in order.

## Variations

• The order is reversed.

• The directional instructions are combined with different spin variations (e.g., slice, topspin).

• The directional instructions are combined with different height and tempo variations.

• The number of given strokes is increased.

## 5.6.9 Backhand Precision

### Set-up

The playing court is divided into areas A, B, C, and D. Each field is again divided into plus and minus, where plus always means outward toward the sideline and minus always means inward toward the centre. Player S is at the baseline. Coach T is standing near the T-line. Sufficient balls are needed.

### Execution

The coach gives the player four stroke variations (e.g., ball one: BH down the line on A+, ball two: BH cross-court on D-, ball three: BH down the line on A+, ball four: BH down the line on C+). The player memorises the coach's instructions and plays the targets in order.

### Variations

- The order is reversed.

- The directional instructions are combined with different cut variations (e.g., slice, topspin).

- The directional instructions are combined with different height and tempo variations.

- The number of given strokes is increased.

# 5.6.10 Volley Precision

1. Attack on A, volley to D

### Set-up
Two players, A and B, position themselves, each on their side, centred on the baseline. Sufficient balls are needed.

### Execution
Coach T plays a ball to the T-line, with which the attacking player A immediately comes to the net. Defending player B should try to play the ball just over the net so the attacking player can place his volley well. If this is successful, the players move back to their starting positions. After the fifth repetition, the point is played out, and the players change their tasks.

### Variations
* Different directions or height variations are given, which the player must remember.

* Different pace and length variations are given.

* Hoops or cones in different colours are placed on the court, which the player must hit in a particular order.

## 5.6.11 Overhead Precision

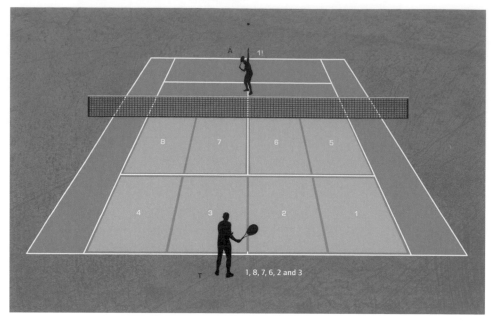

### Set-up

The court is divided into eight fields. Player A is at the net. Coach T stands behind the baseline. Good balls are needed.

### Execution

The coach gives the player six numbers to remember (e.g., eight, seven, six, two, and three). Then he plays six lobs, which the player is supposed to hit to the target fields according to the given order. The player should announce aloud the number of the area he is playing to before he hits the smash.

### Variations

- The order is reversed.

- The number of given fields is increased.

- The coding is changed (e.g., one means eight, three means five).

## 5.6.12 Master of Numbers

### Set-up

Six signal lights (the colours set can be freely chosen), enough balls, and six hoops are needed. The six hoops are distributed randomly on the opponent's side of the court, and a signal light is placed in each hoop. Coach T stands at the side and passes the balls.

### Execution

A random number of signal lights light up briefly at the same time. The player should recognise how many there were. For example, if he sees four signal lights light up, he shouts, "Four!" The coach will pass him four balls with which he should try to hit to those hoops where a signal light has lit up.

### Variations

- The signal lamps light up in random order, one after the other. The player must remember them and hit the hoops in the same order.

- In this variation, the signal lights must be set in four different colours, and four hoops of the same colour are needed.

- The signal lights are placed in a row at the net on the player's half of the court, and the hoops are distributed on the opponent's half of the court.

- The signal lights go on in turn in different colours; the player must remember the order in which the lights went on and try to hit the rings in this order.

# 5.6.13 Even or Odd

## Set-up

Coach T positions himself near the T-line with enough balls. Player A stands at the baseline.

## Execution

The coach feeds balls, always saying a number. All even numbers mean that A has to play down the line, and all odd numbers indicate that A has to play cross-court.

## Variations

- The meanings of even and odd numbers are reversed.

- Straightforward math problems are given. The result is either an even or odd number and triggers a game task for the player (e.g., 8 − 4 = 4 = even = down the line). Addition, subtraction, multiplication, and division can be considered arithmetic problems.

- The exercise can be made more difficult by having the player remember the results of the arithmetic problems and add them up (e.g., if the addition results in a number greater than 20, then the coding is reversed).

    ■ Task one: $2 \times 3 = 6$ = even = down the line

    ■ Task two: $5 + 4 = 9 + 6$ (result of task 1) $= 15$ = odd = cross court

    ■ Task three: $9 - 3 = 6 + 15$ (sum of task 1 and 2) $= 21$ = greater than 20 = odd = down the line

# 5.6.14 Carousel of Colours

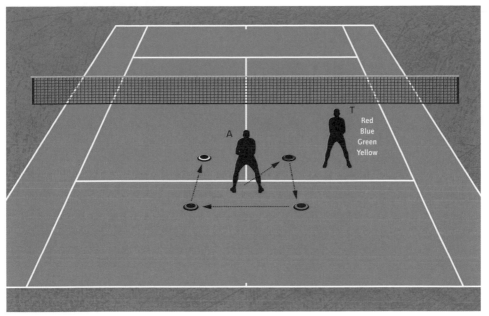

## Set-up

Four signal lights (set colours, four different lights) are needed. The signal lights lie on the floor but can also be raised. The distance between the signal lights depends on the player's size and level. The player is located between the signal lights.

## Execution

Coach T gives the player a colour code (e.g., red, blue, green, yellow). The player must memorise this information. Then the signal lamps light up, and the player has to turn off the lights as fast as possible, in the order given by the coach.

## Variations

* The different colours are assigned certain body parts with which the signal light is put out (e.g., if the red light is on, this is to be wiped out with the right hand, the yellow light with the left hand, the blue light with the right foot, and the green light with the left foot).

* Two other colours are set, which trigger specific tasks for the player. For example, if the signal light is orange, the athlete must turn around once, and if the light is purple, he must clap his hands.

## 5.6.15 Memorise the Colour Pairs

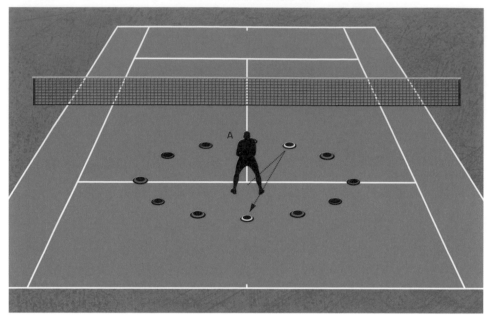

### Set-up

Twelve signal lights (six pairs of colours are to be programmed) are on the floor but can also be elevated on poles. The spacing of the signal lights is based on the size and level of the player. The player is placed between the signal lights.

### Execution

The player is inside the signal light circle. All twelve lights come on simultaneously and are always programmed to create colour pairs. The athlete is supposed to wipe out the colour pairs with his foot or hand one after the other as fast as possible.

### Variations

*   One signal light is to be wiped out with the left hand, while the other light, which is lit in the same colour, is to be wiped out with the right hand.

*   One signal light is to be wiped out with the left foot, while the other light, which is lit in the same colour, is to be wiped out with the right foot.

## 5.6.16 Remember the Code

### Set-up

Eight markers are laid out on one half of the tennis court. Player A is positioned centrally behind the baseline.

### Execution

Player A is told five numbers by coach T, which must be remembered in the correct order. After the start signal, A must approach the markers in the correct order and execute a shadow stroke each time.

### Variation

- The order is reversed.

- The number of given squares is increased.

- The coding is changed (e.g., one means eight, three means five).

## 5.6.17 Hit the Zone

### Set-up

The court is divided into zones, as shown in the illustration. Coach T stands behind player A, while B stands on the opposite side.

### Execution

Coach T tells the player into which zones the ball should be played in the rally (e.g., set the serve with slice wide and the first ball into the opponent's forehand).

## Variations

* The target fields are re-coded using colours and symbols.

* The player must remember several if-then scenarios. For example, the coach gives the following specification: "Serve to the outside on the advantage side with a lot of topspin. If the return comes down the line, then play the ball down the line back with your forehand; if the ball is returned cross-court, then play the ball back cross court. If the ball is returned as a slice, then play a drop-shot."

* The number of given shots and if-then scenarios is increased and given for two, three, or four rallies in advance so that the demand on the player's working memory becomes greater and greater. It is recommended that the coach makes a note of his presets.

## 5.6.18 Light Memory

### Set-up

Ten signal lights are needed. Five are placed just in front of the net on Player A's side. The remaining five signal lights can be positioned anywhere in the opponent's court. Player A is at the net. Coach T stands at the baseline in the opposite court from A. In addition, a helper H is needed to operate the signal light console manually.

### Execution

First, all five signal lights in the opposite field come on and go out after 5 seconds. Player A has to remember which colour lit up where. Then a signal light on A's side of the net goes on (e.g., the green one). A receives a ball from the coach and has to play it on the signal light that was lit in the same colour during the memorisation phase.

## Variations

- The colours of the signal lights in the opposite field are changed after each ball.

- The colours of the signal lights in the opposite field are changed again after each ball. If two signal lights have lit up in the same colour, A must solve a particular game task, such as playing a volley stop.

- If all five signal lights on player A's side light up simultaneously, A is not allowed to play the ball and must let it pass.

# REFERENCES

Abernethy, B. (1990a). Anticipation in squash: Differences in advance cue utilization between expert and novice players. *Journal of sports sciences, 8*, 17-34.

Abernethy, B. (1990b). Expertise, visual search, and information pick-up in squash. *Perception, 19,* 63-77.

Abernethy, B. & Russell, D. G. (1987). Expert-novice differences in an applied selective attention task. *Journal of Sport Psychology, 9,* 326–345.

Abernethy, B., Maxwell, J. P., Masters, R. S. W., van der Kamp, J., & Jackson, R. C. (2007). Attentional processes in skill learning and expert performance. In G. Tenenbaum & R. C. Eklund (Eds.), *Handbook of Sport Psychology* (3rd ed.). New Jersey: Wiley & Sons.

Abernethy, B., Wood, J. M., & Parks, S. (1999). Can the anticipatory skills of experts be learned by novices? *Research Quarterly for Exercise and Sport, 70,* 313–318.

Alvarez, G. A., & Franconeri, S. L. (2005). How many objects can you track? Evidence for a flexible tracking resource. *Journal of Vision, 5,* 641–641.

Alvarez, J. A., & Emory, E. (2006). Executive function and the frontal lobes: a meta-analytic review. *Neuropsychology Review, 16,* 17–42.

Baddeley, A. D. (2007). *Working Memory, Thought, and Action.* Oxford: Oxford. University Press.

Bakker, F. C., Oudejans, R. D., Binsch, O. & van der Kamp, J. (2006). Penalty taking and gaze behaviour: Unwanted effects of the wish not to miss. *International Journal of Sport Psychology, 37,* 265-280.

Beck, D. M., & Lavie, N. (2005). Look here but ignore what you see: effects of distractors at fixation. *Journal of Experimental Psychology: Human Perception and Performance, 31*, 592.

Beilock, S. L., Carr, T. H., MacMahon, C. & Starkes, J. L. (2002). When paying attention becomes counterproductive: Impact of divided versus skill-focused attention of novice and experienced performance of sensorimotor skills. *Journal of Experimental Psychology: Applied, 8*, 6-16.

Bishop, D. T., Wright, M. J., Jackson, R. C., & Abernethy, B. (2013). Neural bases for anticipation skill in soccer: an FMRI study. *Journal of Sport & Exercise Psychology, 35*, 98-109.

Broadbent, D. E. (1958). *Perception and communication*. London: Pergamon Press.

Bruce, V., Green, P., & Georgeson, M. (1996). *Visual perception. Physiology, psychology and ecology* (3ʳᵈ ed.). Hove: Psychology Press.

Caserta, R. J. & Singer, R. N. (2004). The effectiveness of video situational awareness learning in response to video tennis match situations. *Journal of Sport & Exercise Psychology*, 26, 48-49.

Cauraugh, J. H. & Janelle, C. M. (2002). Visual search and cue utilisation in racket sports. In K. Davids, G. J. P. Savelsbergh, S. J. Bennett & J. Van Der Kamp (Eds.), *Interceptive Actions in Sport* (pp. 64–89). London: Routledge.

Cavanagh, P., & Alvarez, G.A. (2005). Tracking multiple targets with multifocal attention. *Trends in Cognitive Sciences, 9*, 349–354.

Cohen, M. A., Nakayama, K., Konkle, T., Stantic, M., & Alvarez, G. A. (2015). Visual awareness is limited by the representational architecture of the visual system. *Journal of Cognitive Neuroscience, 27*, 2240-2252.

Conway, A. R. A., Jarrold, C., Kane, M. J., Miyake, A., & Towse, J. N. (2007). *Variation in Working Memory*. New York: Oxford University Press.

Conway, A. R., Kane, M. J., Bunting, M. F., Hambrick, D. Z., Wilhelm, O., & Engle, R. W. (2005). Working memory span tasks: A methodological review and user's guide. *Psychonomic Bulletin & Review, 12*, 769-786.

Côté, J., Baker, J., & Abernethy, B. (2007). Practice and play in the development of sport expertise. In G. Tenenbaum & R.C. Eklund (Eds.), *Handbook of Sport Psychology* (pp. 184-202) Hoboken, NJ.: Wiley.

Coull, J. T. (1998). Neural correlates of attention and arousal: Insights from electrophysiology, functional neuroimaging and psychopharmacology. *Progress in Neurobiology*, 55, 343–361.

Cowan, N. (1995) *Attention and Memory: An integrated framework.* New York: Oxford University Press.

Cowan, N. (2001). The magical number 4 in short-term memory: A reconsideration of mental storage capacity. *Behavioural and Brain Sciences 24*, 87–185. doi:10.1017/S0140525X01003922

Cowan, N. (2005). *Working memory capacity.* Hove, East Sussex, UK: Psychology Press.

Crone, E. A., Wendelken, C., Donohue, S., van Leijenhorst, L. & Bunge, S. A. (2006). Neurocognitive development of the ability to manipulate information in working memory. *Proc. Natl. Acad. Sci. U.S.A. 103*, 9315-9320. doi: 10.1073/ pnas.0510088103

Del Villar, F., González, L. G., Iglesias, D., Moreno, M. P. & Cervelló, E. M. (2007). Expert-novice differences in cognitive and execution skills during tennis competition. *Perceptual and Motor Skills, 104*, 355-365.

Diamond, A. (2013). Executive functions. *Annual Review of Psychology, 64*, 135-168.

Dicks, M., Button, C. & Davids, K. (2010). Availability of advanced visual information constrains association-football goalkeeping performance during penalty kicks. *Perception, 39*, 1111–1124.

Dietrich, K. (1984). Vermitteln Spielreihen die Spielfähigkeit? *Sportpädagogik, 8*, 19–21.

Döbler, H. (1964). Die Systematik der Spiele als Grundlage einer vergleichenden sportpädagogischen Betrachtung. *Theorie und Praxis der Körperkultur, 13*, 217-231.

Ekblom, B. (1986). Applied physiology of soccer. *Sports Medicine, 3*, 50-60.

Engle, R.W. (2002). Working memory capacity as executive attention. Current directions. *Psychological science, 11(1)*, 19-23.

Ericsson, K. A., Krampe, R. T. & Tesch-Römer, C. (1993). The role of deliberate practice in the acquisition of expert performance. *Psychological Review, 100*, 363-406.

Eriksen, C. W., & St. James, J. D. (1986). Visual attention within and around the field of focal attention: A zoom lens model. *Perception & Psychophysics, 40*, 225–240. doi:10.3758/BF03211502

Farrow, D., & Abernethy, B. (2002). Can anticipatory skills be learned through implicit video-based perceptual training? *Journal of Sports Science, 20*, 471-485.

Farrow, D., & Abernethy, B. (2007). Wahrnehmung von Expertinnen und Experten im Sport: Einige Kernfragen und -probleme. In N. Hagemann, M. Tietjens, & B. Strauß (Hrsg.), *Psychologie der sportlichen Höchstleistung* (S. 71–92). Göttingen: Hogrefe.

Fink, A., Rominger, C., Benedek, M., Perchtold, C. M., Papousek, I., Weiss, E. M., … & Memmert, D. (2018). EEG alpha activity during imagining creative moves in soccer decision-making situations. *Neuropsychologia, 114,* 118-124.

Fink, A., Bay, J. U., Koschutnig, K., Prettenthaler, K., Rominger, C., Benedek, M., … & Memmert, D. (2019). Brain and soccer: Functional patterns of brain activity during the generation of creative moves in real soccer decision-making situations. *Human Brain Mapping, 40,* 755-764. [3.14]

Fernández-García, Á. I., Blanca-Torres, J. C., Nikolaidis, P. T. & Torres-Luque, G. (2019). Differences in competition statistics between winners and losers in male and female tennis players in Olympic Games. *German Journal of Exercise and Sport Research,49,* 313.

Friedman, N. P., Miyake, A., Corley, R. P., Young, S. E., DeFries, J. C. & Hewitt, J. K. (2006). Not all executive functions are related to intelligence. *Psychological Science, 17,* 172-179.

Friedrich, W. (2005). *Optimales Sportwissen.* Spitta Verlag GmbH & Co. KG.

Furley, P., & Memmert, D. (2010). The role of working memory in sports. *International Review of Sport and Exercise Psychology, 3,* 171–194.

Furley, P., & Memmert, D. (2012). Working Memory Capacity as controlled attention in tactical decision making. *Journal of Sport and Exercise Psychology, 34,* 322–344.

Furley, P., & Memmert, D. (2013). "Whom should I pass to?" The more options the more attentional guidance from working. *PLOS ONE 8*: e62278. doi: 10.1371/journal.pone.0062278

Furley, P., & Memmert, D. (2015). Creativity and Working Memory Capacity in Sports: Working Memory Capacity Is not a Limiting Factor in Creative Decision Making amongst Skilled Performers. *Frontiers in Psychology.* doi: 10.3389/fpsyg.2015.00115

Furley, P., Memmert, D., & Heller, C. (2010). The dark side of visual awareness in sport – inattentional blindness in a real-world basketball task. *Attention, Perception & Psychophysics, 72,* 1327–1337.

Furley, P., Memmert, D. & Schmid, S. (2013). Perceptual load in sport and the heuristic value of the perceptual load paradigm in examining expertise related perceptual-cognitive adaptations. *Cognitive Processing, 14*, 31-42.

Furley, P., Schul, K, & Memmert, D. (2017). Das Experten-Novizen-Paradigma und die Vertrauenskrise in der Psychologie. *Zeitschrift für Sportpsychologie, 23*, 131–140. doi:10.1026/1612-5010/a000174

García-González, L., Iglesias, D., Moreno, A., Moreno, M. P. & Del Villar, F. (2012). Tactical knowledge in tennis: A comparison of two groups with different levels of expertise. *Perceptual and Motor Skills, 115*, 567-580.

García-González, L., Moreno, A., Gil, A., Moreno, M. P. & Villar, F. D. (2014). Effects of decision training on decision making and performance in young tennis players: An applied research. *Journal of Applied Sport Psychology, 26*, 426-440.

Goulet, C., Bard, C. & Fleury, M. (1989). Expertise differences in preparing to return a tennis serve: A visual information processing approach. *Journal of Sport & Exercise Psychology, 11*, 382-398.

Gray, R. (2004). Attending to the execution of a complex sensorimotor skill: Expertise differences, choking, and slumps. *Journal of Experimental Psychology: Applied, 10*, 42-54.

Guilford, J. P. (1967). *The nature of human intelligence.* New York: McGraw-Hill.

Guillot, A., Desliens, S., Rouyer, C. & Rogowski, I. (2013). Motor imagery and tennis serve performance: the external focus efficacy. *Journal of Sports Science & Medicine, 12*, 332.

Güldenpenning, I., Braun, J. F., Machlitt, D. & Schack, T. (2015). Masked priming of complex movements: perceptual and motor processes in unconscious action perception. *Psychological Research, 79*, 801-812.

Güldenpenning, I., Kunde, W. & Weigelt, M. (2017). How to trick your opponent: A review article on deceptive actions in interactive sports. *Frontier in Psychology, 8*, 917.

Güldenpenning, I., Steinke, A., Koester, D. & Schack, T. (2013). Athletes and novices are differently capable to recognize feint and non-feint actions. *Experimental Brain Research, 230*, 333-343.

Hadler, R., Chiviacowsky, S., Wulf, G. & Schild, J. F. G. (2014). Children's learning of tennis skills is facilitated by external focus instructions. *Motriz: Revista de Educação Física, 20*, 418-422.

Hagemann, N. & Loffing, F. (2013). Antizipation. In A. Güllich & M. Krüger (Hrsg.), *Sport. Das Lehrbuch für das Sportstudium* (S. 562-564). Berlin: Springer.

Hagemann, N. & Memmert, D. (2006). Coaching anticipatory skill in badminton: Laboratory- versus field-based perceptual training? *Journal of Human Movements Studies, 50*, 381-398.

Hambrick, D. Z. & Meinz, E. J. (2011). Limits on the predictive power of domain-specific experience and knowledge in skilled performance. *Current Directions in Psychological Science, 20*, 275-279.

Hambrick, D. Z., Burgoyne, A. P. & Oswald, F. L. (2019). Domain-general models of expertise: The role of cognitive ability. In P. Ward, J. M. Schraagen, J. Gore & E. Roth (Eds.), *Oxford handbook of expertise: Research and application (p.1-40)*. Oxford: Oxford UP.

Harris, D., Wilson, M. R. & Vine, S. J. (2018). A systematic review of commercial cognitive training devices: Implications for use in sport. *Frontiers in Psychology, 9*, 709.

Herzog, H. D. (1986). Zur Theoriearbeit im taktischen Training der Sportspiele. *Wissenschaftliche Zeitschrift der DHfK Leipzig, 27*, 73-84.

Höner, O. (2005). *Entscheidungshandeln im Sportspiel Fußball: eine Analyse im Lichte der Rubikontheorie*. Hofmann: Schorndorf.

Huesmann, K. & Loffing, F. (2019). Contextual cue utilization in visual anticipation in tennis: On the role of an opponent's on-court position and skill. *German Journal of Exercise and Sport Research, 49*, 304-312.

Hüttermann, S., Memmert, D., Simons, D. J. & Bock, O. (2013). Fixation strategy influences the ability to focus attention on two spatially separate objects. *PLoS ONE, 8*, e65673.

Hüttermann, S., Noël, B. & Memmert, D. (2017). Evaluating erroneous offside calls in soccer. *PloS one, 12*, e0174358.

Hüttermann, S., Noël, B. & Memmert, D. (2018). Eye tracking in high-performance sports: Evaluation of its application in expert athletes. *International Journal of Computer Science in Sport, 17*, 182-203.

Hüttermann, S., Simons, D. & Memmert, D. (2014). The size and shape of the attentional "spotlight" vary with differences in sports expertise. *Journal of Experimental Psychology: Applied, 20,* 147-157.

Huys, R., Cañal-Burland, R., Hagemann, H., Beek, P. P., Smeeton, N. J.& Williams, A. M. (2009). Global information pickup underpins anticipation of tennis shot direction. *Journal of Motor Behavior, 41, 158-171.*

Intriligator, J. & Cavanagh, P. (2001). The spatial resolution of visual attention. *Cognitive psychology, 43,* 171-216.

Jackson, R. C. & Farrow, D. (2005). Implicit perceptual training: How, when, and why?. Human Movement Science, 24, 308-325.

Jackson, R. C. & Mogan, P. (2010). Advance visual information, awareness, and anticipation skill. *Journal of Motor Behavior, 39, 341-351.*

Jackson, R. C., Warren, S. & Abernethy, B. (2006). Anticipation skill and susceptibility to deceptive movements. *Acta Psychology, 123,* 355-371.

Kane, M. J., Hambrick, D. Z., Tuholski, S. W., Wilhelm, O., Payne, T. W. & Engle, R. W. *(2004)*. The generality of working memory capacity: a latent-variable approach to verbal and visuospatial memory span and reasoning. *Journal of Experimental Psychology: General, 133,* 189.

Kempe, M. & Memmert, D. (2018). "Good, better, creative": the influence of creativity on goal scoring in elite soccer. *Journal of Sports Sciences,* 1-5.

Klingberg, T. (2010). Training and plasticity of working memory. *Trends in cognitive sciences, 14,* 317-324.

Knudsen, E. (2007). Fundamental components of attention. *Annual Review of Neuroscience, 30,* 57-78.

König, S. & Memmert, D. (2021, in press). Taktik und Taktiktraining im Sport – Anwendungsbereiche, Diagnostik, Trainingsformen, Organisation, Methoden, Anpassungen. In M. Fröhlich & A. Güllich (Eds.), *Sportmotorik, Bewegung und Training.* Berlin: Springer.

König, S. (1997). Zur Vermittlung von Spielfähigkeit in der Schule. *Sportunterricht, 46,* 476-486.

Konzag, I. & Konzag, G. (1980). Anforderungen an die kognitiven Funktionen in der psychischen Regulation sportlicher Spielhandlungen. *Theorie und Praxis der Körperkultur, 29*, 20-31.

Kredel, R., Vater, C., Klostermann, A. & Hossner, E. (2017). Eye-tracking technology and the dynamics of natural gaze behaviour in sports: A systematic review of 40 years of research. *Frontiers in Psychology, 8*, 1-15.

Kröger, C. & Roth, K. (1999). *Ballschule – Ein ABC für Spielanfänger.* Schorndorf: Hofmann.

Kuhlmann, D. (1989). Wie führt man Spiele ein? In Bielefelder & Sportpädagogen (Hrsg.), *Methoden im Sportunterricht* (S. 135- 148). Schorndorf: Hofmann.

LaBerge, D. (1983). Spatial extent of attention to letters and words. *Journal of Experimental Psychology: Human Perception and Performance, 9*, 371-379.

Lees, A. (2019). The evolution of racket sport since- a personal reflection. *German Journal of Exercise and Sport Research, 49*, 213-220.

Loffing, F., Cañal-Bruland, R. & Hagemann, N. (2014). Antizipationstraining im Sport. In K. Zentgraf, & J. Munzert (Hrsg..). *Kognitives Training im Sport* (S. 137-161). Göttingen: Hogrefe Verlag.

Loffing, F., Hagemann, N. & Farrow, D (2017). Perceptual-cognitive training: The next piece of the puzzle. In J. Baker, S. Cobley, J. Schorer & N. Wattie (Eds.), *Routledge handbook of talent identification and development in sport* (pp. 207-220). London: Routledge.

Luciana, M., Conklin, H. M., Hooper, C. J. & Yarger, R. S. (2005). The development of nonverbal working memory and executive control processes in adolescents. *Child Development, 76*, 697-712.

Mack, A. & Rock, I. (1998). *Inattentional blindness.* MIT Press: Cambridge.

MacNamara, B. N., Hambrick, D. Z. & Oswald, F. L. (2014). Deliberate practice and performance in music, games, sports, education, and professions: A meta-analysis *Psychological Science, 25*, 1608-1618.

Magill, R. A. (1998). Knowledge is more than we can talk about: Implicit learning in motor skill acquisition. *Research Quarterly for Exercise and Sport, 69*, 104-110.

Mann, D. T., Williams, A. M. Ward, P. &Janelle, C. M. (2007). Perceptual-cognitive expertise in sport: a meta-analysis. *Journal of Sport & Exercise Psychology. 29*, 457-478.

Marr, D. (1982). *Vision: A computational investigation into the human representation and processing of visual information.* San Francisco: Freeman.

Masters, R. S. W., van der Kamp, J. & Jackson, R. C. (2007). Imperceptibly off-center goalkeepers influence penalty-kick direction in soccer. *Psychological Science, 18,* 222-223.

Maxwell, J. P., Masters, R. S. & Eves, F. F. (2003). The role of working memory in motor learning and performance. *Consciousness and Cognition, 12,* 376-402.

McPherson, S. L. & Thomas, J. R. (1989). Relation of knowledge and performance in boys' tennis: Age and expertise. *Journal of Experimental Child Psychology, 48,* 190-211.

Meffert, D., O'Shannessy, C., Born, P., Grambow, R. & Vogt, T. (2019). Tennis at tiebreaks: addressing elite players' performance for tomorrows' coaching. *German Journal of Exercise and Sport Research, 49,* 339-344.

Meier, C., Fett, J. & Gröben, B. (2019). The influence of analogy instruction and motion rule instruction on the learning process of junior tennis players. Qualitative assessment of serve performance. *German Journal of Exercise and Sport Research, 49,* 291-303.

Memmert, D. (2004a). *Kognitionen im Sportspiel.* Köln: Sport & Buch Strauß.

Memmert, D. (2004b). Ein Forschungsprogramm zur Validierung sportspielübergreifender Basistaktiken. *Sportwissenschaft, 34,* 341-354.

Memmert, D. (2005). Ich sehe was, was du nicht siehst!" – Das Phänomen Inattentional Blindness im Sport. *Leistungssport, 5,* 11-15.

Memmert, D. (2006). Wann soll man spezialisieren? – Kreativität als Indikator auf der 1. und 2. Stufe des MSIL. In K. Weber, D. Augustin, P. Maier & K. Roth (Hrsg.). *Wissenschaftlicher Transfer für die Praxis: Ausbildung – Training – Wettkampf* (S. 59-64). Köln: Sport & Buch Strauß.

Memmert, D. (2007). Can creativity be improved by an attention-broadening training program? – An exploratory study focusing on team sports. *Creativity Research Journal, 19,* 281-292.

Memmert, D. (2009). Pay attention! A review of attentional expertise in sport. *International Review of Sport & Exercise Psychology, 2,* 119-138.

Memmert, D. (2010a). Creativity, Expertise, and Attention: Exploring their Development and their Relationships. *Journal of Sport Science, 29,* 93-104.

Memmert, D. (2010b). Testing of tactical performance in youth elite soccer. *Journal of Sports Science & Medicine, 9*, 199-205.

Memmert, D. (2012). Kreativität im Sportspiel. *Sportwissenschaft 42*, 38-49.

Memmert, D. (2013). Leistungsfaktoren im Sportspiel. In A. Güllich & M. Krüger (Hrsg.), Sport - *Das Lehrbuch für das Sportstudium* (S. 561-562). Berlin: Springer Verlag.

Memmert, D. (2015). *Teaching tactical creativity in team and racket sports: Research and Practice.* Abingdon: Routledge.

Memmert, D. (2017a). Tactical creativity in sport. In J. Kaufman, V. Glăveanu & J. Baer (Eds.), *The Cambridge handbook of creativity across domains* (pp. 479491). Cambridge: Cambridge University Press. doi:10.1017/9781316274385.026

Memmert, D. (2017b). Sports and creativity. M. A. Runco and S. R. Pritzker (Eds.) *Encyclopedia of creativity,* (2nd ed.), (pp. 373-378). San Diego: Academic Press.

Memmert, D. & Breihofer, P. (2006). *Doppelstunde Fußball.* Schorndorf: Hofmann.

Memmert, D. & Furley, P. (2007). "I spy with my little eye!" – b-eadth of attention, inattentional blindness, and tactical decision making in team sports. *Journal of Sport & Exercise Psychology, 29*, 365–347.

Memmert, D. & Furley, P. (2012). Aufmerksamkeit. M. Krüger & A. Güllich (Hrsg.), *Bachelor-Kurs Sport. Ein Lehrbuch für das Studium der Sportwissenschaft (S. 567-568).* Berlin: Springer-Verlag.

Memmert, D. & König, S. (2011). Zur Vermittlung einer allgemeinen Spielfähigkeit im Sportspiel. In S. König, D. Memmert & K. Moosmann. *Das große Buch der Sportspiele* (S. 18-37). Wiebelsheim: Limpert-Verlag.

Memmert, D. & Roth, K. (2003). Individualtaktische Leistungsdiagnostik im Sportspiel. *Spektrum der Sportwissenschaft, 15*, 44-70.

Memmert, D. & Roth, K. (2007). The effects of non-specific and specific concepts on tactical creativity in team ball sports. *Journal of Sports Sciences, 25*, 1423-1432.

Memmert, D., Baker, J. & Bertsch, C. (2010). Play and practice in the development of sport-specific creativity in team ball sports. *High Ability Studies, 21*, 3-18.

Memmert, D., Hagemann, H., Althoetmar, R. Geppert, S. & Seiler, D. (2009). Conditions of practice in perceptual skill learning. *Research Quarterly for Exercise & Sport, 80*, 32-43.

Memmert, D., Hüttermann, S. & Orliczek, J. (2013). Decide like Lionel Messi! The impact of regulatory focus on divergent thinking in sports. *Journal of Applied Social Psychology, 43,* 2163-2167.

Memmert, D., Hüttermann, S. & Kreitz, C. (2019 im Druck). Wahrnehmung und Aufmerksamkeit. In J. Schüler, M. Wegner & H. Plessner (Hrsg.), *Lehrbuch Sportpsychologie – Theoretische Grundlagen und Anwendung.* Berlin: Springer.

Memmert, D., Thumfart, M. & Uhing, M. (2014). *Optimales Taktiktraining im Kinder-, Jugend- und Leistungsfußball.* Balingen: Spitta Verlag.

Mirsky, A. F., Anthony, B. J., Duncan, C. C, Ahearn, M. B. & Kellam, S. G. (1991). Analysis of the elements of attention: A neuropsychological approach. *Neuropsychological Review, 2,* 109-145.

Moran, A. P. (1996). *The psychology of concentration in sport performers: A cognitive analysis.* Hove: Psychology Press.

Most, S. B., Scholl, B. J., Clifford, E. R. & Simons, D. J. (2005). What you see is what you set: Sustained inattentional blindness and the capture of awareness. *Psychological Review, 112,* 217-242.

Myers, N. L., Kibler, W. B., Axtell, A. H., Herde, B. J., Westgate, P. M. & Uhl, T. L.(2019). Musculoskeletal capacity and serve mechanics in professional women's tennis players. *German Journal of Exercise and Sport Research, 49,* 275-284.

Neisser, U. (2014). *Cognitive psychology.* Classic edition: Psychology Press.

Noël, B., van der Kamp, J. & Memmert, D. (2015). Implicit goalkeeper influences on goal side selection in representative penalty kicking tasks. *PLoS ONE, 10,* e01354423.

Noël, B., van der Kamp, J., Masters, R. & Memmert, D. (2016). Scan direction influences explicit but not implicit perception of a goalkeeper's position. *Attention, Perception & Psychophysics.* doi: 10.3758/s13414-016-1196-2

Noël, B., van der Kamp, J., Weigelt, M. & Memmert, D. (2015). Asymmetries in spatial perception are more prevalent under explicit than implicit attention. *Consciousness and Cognition, 34,* 10-15.

Owen, A. M., Hampshire, A., Grahn, J. A., Stenton, R., Dajani, S., Burns, A. S. & Ballard, C. G. (2010). Putting brain training to the test. *Nature, 465*(7299), 775.

Posner, M. I. (1980). Orienting of attention. *Quarterly Journal of Experimental Psychology, 32*, 3-25. doi:10.1080/00335558008248231

Posner, M. I. & Boies, S. J. (1971). Components of attention. *Psychological Review, 78*, 391-408.

Posner, M. I. & Peterson, S. E. (1990). The attention system of the human brain. *Annual Review of Neuroscience, 13*, 25-42.

Prinz, W. (1997). Perception and action planning. *European Journal of Cognitive Psychology, 9*, 129-154.

Raschke, A. & Lames, M. (2019). Video-based tactic training in tennis. Proof of effiacy in a field experiment with 10- to 14-year-old tournament players. *German Journal of Exercise and Sport Research, 49*, 345-350.

Ripoll, H. & Fleurance, P. (1988). What does keeping one's eye on the ball mean?. *Ergonomics, 31*, 1647-1654.

Roca, A., Memmert, D., & Ford, P. R. (2018). Creative Decision Making and Visual Search Behaviour in Skilled Soccer Players. *PloS one, 13(7)*, e0199381.

Roca, A., Ford, P.R. & Memmert, D. (2020). Perceptual-cognitive processes underlying creative expert performance in soccer. *Psychological Research*, 1-10.

Romeas, T., Guldner, A., & Faubert, J. (2016). 3D-multiple object tracking training task improves passing decision-making accuracy in soccer players. *Psychology of Sport and Exercise, 22*, 1-9.

Rominger, C., Memmert, D., Papousek, I., Perchtold, C. M., Weiss, E. M., Benedek, M., Schwerdtfeger, A. R., & Fink, A. (2020). Different neurocognitive strategies in women and men in generating creative solutions in soccer decision-making situations. *Psychology of Sport & Exercise, 50*, 101748.

Rominger, C., Memmert, D., Papousek, I., Perchtold, C. M., Weiss, E. M., Benedek, M., Schwerdtfeger, A. R., & Fink, A. (2021). Brain activation during the observation of real soccer game situations predict creative goalscoring. *Social Cognitive and Affective Neuroscience*.

Roth, G. & Menzel, R. (2001). Neuronale Grundlagen kognitiver Leistungen. In J. Dudel, R. Menzel & R. F. Schmidt (Hrsg.), *Neurowissenschaft. Vom Molekül zur Kognition* (S. 543-563). Berlin: Springer.

Roth, K. (2005). Taktiktraining. In A. Hohmann, M. Kolb & K. Roth (Hrsg.), *Handbuch Sportspiel* (S. 342-349). Schorndorf: Hofmann.

Roth, K. & Hossner, E. J. (1999). Die funktionalen Betrachtungsweisen. In K. Roth & K. Willimczik (Hrsg.), *Bewegungswissenschaft* (S. 127-225). Reinbek: Rowohlt.

Roth, K. & Kröger, C. (2011). *Ballschule. Ein ABC für Spielanfänger* (4. Aufl.). Schorndorf: Hofmann.

Roth, K., Kröger, Ch. & Memmert, D. (2002). *Ballschule Rückschlagspiele.* Schorndorf: Hofmann.

Roth, K., Memmert, D. & Schubert, R. (2006). *Ballschule Wurfspiele.* Schorndorf: Hofmann.

Rowe, R., Horswill, M. S., Kronvall-Parkinson, M., Poulter, D. R. & McKenna, F. P. (2009). The effect of disguise on novice expert tennis players' anticipation ability. *Journal of Applied Sport Psychology, 21, 178-185.*

Savelsbergh, G. J. P., van Gastel, P. J. & van Kampen, P. M. (2010). Anticipation of penalty kicking direction can be improved by directing attention through perceptual learning. *International Journal of Sport Psychology, 41,* 24-41.

Scharfen, E. & Memmert, D. (2019a). Measurement of cognitive functions in experts and elite-athletes: A meta-analytic review. *Applied Cognitive Psychology. 10.1002/acp.3526.*

Scharfen, E. & Memmert, D. (2019b). The relationship between cognitive functions and sport-specific motor skills in elite youth soccer players. *Frontiers in Psychology – Movement Science & Sport Psychology, 10, 817. doi:10.3389/fpsyg.2019.00817*

Scharfen, H. E., & Memmert, D. (2021) Cognitive training in elite soccer players: evidence of narrow, but not broad transfer to visual and executive function. *German Journal of Exercise and Sport Research,* 1-11.

Schmidt, R. A. & Wrisberg, C. A. (2004). *Motor learning and performance. A problem-based learning approach* (3rd ed). Champaign: Human Kinetics.

Schnabel, G. & Thieß, G. (Hrsg.). (1993). *Lexikon Sportwissenschaft – Leistung – Training – Wettkampf.* Berlin: Sportverlag.

Shim, J., Carlton, L. G. & Kwon, Y. H. (2006). Perception of kinematic characteristics of tennis strokes for anticipating stroke type and direction. *Research Quarterly for Exercises and Sport, 77, 326-339.*

Shim, J., Carlton, L. G., Chow, J. W. & Chae, W. S. (2010). The use of anticipatory visual cues by highly skilled tennis players. *Journal of Motor Behavior, 37, 164-175.*

Shim, J., Miller, G. & Lutz, R. (2005). Visual cues and information used to anticipate tennis ball shots and placement. *Journal of Sport Behavior, 28, 186-200.*

Simons, D. J., Boot, W. R., Charness, N., Gathercole, S. E., Chabris, C. F., Hambrick, D. Z. & Stine-Morrow, E. A. (2016). Do "brain-training" programs work? *Psychological Science in the Public Interest, 17,* 103-186.

Singer, R. N., Cauraugh, J. H., Chen, D., Steinberg, G. M. & Frehlich, S. G. (1996). Visual search, anticipation, and reactive comparisons between highly-skilled and beginning tennis players. *Journal of Applied Sport Psychology, 8,* 9-26.

Smeeton, N. J. & Williams, A. M. (2012). The role of movement exaggeration in anticipation of deceptive soccer penalty kicks. *British Journal of Psychology. 103,* 539-555.

Smeeton, N. J., Williams, A. M., Hodges, N. J. & North, J. (2004). Developing perceptual skills in tennis through explicit, guided-discovery, and discovery methods. *Journal of Sport & Exercise Psychology, 24(Suppl.),* 175.

Smeeton, N. J. & Huys, R. (2011). Anticipation of tennis-shot direction from whole-body movement: The role of movement amplitude and dynamics. *Human Movement Science, 30, 957-965.*

Söğüt, M., Luz, L. G., Kaya, Ö. B. & Altunsoy, K. (2019). Ranking in young tennis players—a study to determine possible correlates. *German Journal of Exercise and Sport Research, 49,* 325-331.

Spencer, M. R. & Gastin, P. B. (2001). Energy system contribution during 200-to 1500-m running in highly trained athletes. *Medicine & Science in Sports & Exercise, 33,* 157-162.

Stiehler, G., Konzag, I. & Döbler, H. (1988). *Sportspiele. Theorie und Methodik der Sportspiele Basketball – Fußball – Handball – Volleyball.* Berlin: Sportverlag.

Styles, E. A. (2008). *The psychology of attention.* Hove and New York: Psychology Press.

Tay, C. S., Chow, J. Y., Koh, M. & Button, C. (2012). The effectiveness of keeperindependent penalty kicks using fake visual cues from penalty takers. *International Journal of Sport Psychology. 43,* 403-419.

Tayler, M. A., Burwitz, L. & Davids, K. (1994). Coaching perceptual strategy in badminton. *Journal of Sports Sciences, 12,* 213.

Tenenbaum, G. (2003). Expert athletes: An integrated approach to decision making. In J. L. Starkes & K. A. Ericsson (Eds.), *Expert performance in sports* (pp. 191-218). Champaign, IL: Human Kinetics.

Triolet, C., Benguigui, N., Le Runigo, C. & Williams, A.M. (2013). Quantifying the nature of anticipation in professional tennis. *Journal of Sports Sciences, 31, 820-830.*

Tudos, S., Predoiu, A. & Predoiu, R. (2015). Topographical memory and the concentration of attention in top female tennis players. *Procedia-Social and Behavioral Sciences, 190,* 293-298.

Van Zomeren, A. H. & Brouwer, W. H. (1994). *Clinical neuropsychology of attention.* New York: Oxford University Press.

Verburgh, L., Scherder, E. J., Van Lange, P. A. & Oosterlaan, J. (2016). Do elite and amateur soccer players outperform non-athletes on neurocognitive functioning? A study among 8-12 years old children. *PloS One, 11,* e:0165741. doi:10.1371/journal.pone.0165741

Vestberg, T., Gustafson, R., Maurex, L., Ingvar, M., & Petrovic, P. (2012). Executive functions predict the success of top-soccer players. *PloS one, 7,* e34731. doi:10.1371/journal. pone.0034731

Voss, M. W., Kramer, A. F., Basak, C., Prakash, R. S. & Roberts, B. (2010). Are expert athletes 'expert' in the cognitive laboratory? A metaanalytic review of cognition and sport expertise. *Applied Cognitive Psychology, 24,* 812-826.

Ward, P., Williams, A. M. & Bennett, S. L. (2002). Visual search and biological motion perception in tennis. *Research Quarterly for Exercise and Sport, 73, 107-112.*

Wegner, M. & Katzenberger, C. (1994). Die Spielkonzeption zur Lösung taktischer Problemsituationen: Wissenschaftliche Fundierung eines Trainingsprogramms zum Gegenstoßverhalten im Handball. In R. Brack, A. Hohmann & H. Wieland (Hrsg.), *Trainingssteuerung* (S. 248-253). Stuttgart: Naglschmid.

Weigelt, M., Memmert, D. & Schack, T. (2012). Kick it like Ballack: The effects of goalkeeping gestures on goal-side selection in experienced soccer players and soccer novices. *Journal of Cognitive Psychology, 24,* 942-956.

Williams, A. M. & Ericsson, K. A. (2005). Some considerations when applying the expert performance approach in sport. *Human Movement Science, 24,* 283-307.

Williams, A. M. & Ward, P. (2003). Perceptual expertise: Development in sport. In J. L. Starkes & K. A. Ericsson (Eds.), *Expert performance in sports: Advances in research on sport expertise* (S. 219-249). Champaign, IL: Human Kinetics.

Williams, A. M., Davids, K. & Williams, J. G. (1999). *Visual perception and action in sport.* London: E & F.N Spon.

Williams, A. M., Hodges, N. J., North, J. S. & Barton, G. (2006). Perceiving patterns of play in dynamic sport tasks: identifying the essential information underlying skilled performance. *Perception, 35*, 317-332.

Williams, A. M., Ward, P. & Chapman, C. (2003). Training perceptual skill in field hockey: Is there transfer from the laboratory to the field. *Research Quarterly for Exercise & Sport, 74*, 98-103.

Williams, A. M., Ward, P., Knowles, J. M. & Smeeton, N. J. (2002). Anticipation skill in a real-world task: Measurement, training, and transfer in tennis. *Journal of Experimental Psychology: Applied, 8*, 259-270.

Williams, A. M., Ward, P., Smeeton, N. J. & Allen, D. (2004). Developing anticipation skills in tennis using on-court instruction: Perception versus perception and action. *Journal of Applied Sport Psychology, 16*, 350-360.

Wright, M. J. & Jackson, R. C. (2014). Deceptive body movements reverse spatial cueing in soccer. *PLoS ONE 9*:e104290.

Wulf, G. (2007). *Attention and motor skill learning.* Champaign, IL: Human Kinetics.

Wulf, G., McConnel, N., Gärtner, M. & Schwarz, A. (2002). Feedback and attentional focus: Enhancing the learning of sport skills through external-focus feedback. *Journal of Motor Behavior, 34*, 171-182.

# Credits

Cover design: Anja Elsen

Interior design: Katerina Georgieva, Anja Elsen

Layout: DiTech Publishing Services, www.ditechpubs.com

Cover photo: © AdobeStock

Interior stock images: © AdobeStock

Interior photos: p. 50, 105 © dpa picture alliance; p. 35, 46, 54, 69, 70, 71, 72, 73, 75, 77, 81 © Daniel Memmert

Interior drill diagrams: Mara Schneider

Managing editor: Elizabeth Evans

Copy editor: Anne Rumery

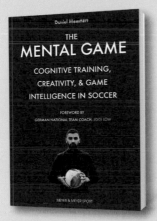